PO GUIDES
TO THE PRIMARY CURRICULUM

ICT

Samantha Uppal

Provides the knowledge you need
to teach the primary curriculum

Author
Samantha Uppal

Editor
Carolyn Gifford

Assistant Editor
David Sandford

Cover design
Joy Monkhouse
Rachel Warner

Designer
Rachael Hammond

Illustrations
Garry Davies
Richard Morris

Cover photograph
Calvin Hewitt

Published by Scholastic Ltd,
Villiers House,
Clarendon Avenue,
Leamington Spa,
Warwickshire CV32 5PR

Text © 2000 Samantha Uppal
© 2000 Scholastic Ltd

1 2 3 4 5 6 7 8 9 0   0 1 2 3 4 5 6 7 8 9

British Library Cataloguing-in-Publication
Data
A catalogue record for this book is
available from the British Library.

ISBN 0-590-53894-2

Every effort has been made to ensure that
websites and addresses referred to in this
book are correct and educationally sound.
They are believed to be current at the
time of publication. The publishers
cannot be held responsible for subsequent
changes in the address of a website, nor
for the content of the sites mentioned.
Referral to a website is not an
endorsement by the publisher of that site.

CONTENTS

ICT

Introduction

The growing use of computers in all walks of life has been mirrored in schools. Pupils often come to school armed with significant amounts of technological expertise that may be a little disconcerting for some teachers. A common response is thankfully not a violent Luddite one but one which seems to dismiss the importance of computers in the hope that they will go away. The situation, however, only underlines the importance of ICT in schools and schools' obligations to deliver ICT to pupils in a technologically driven society.

The newcomer

For many teachers ICT is a completely unknown territory. Memories of it in their own school life do not exist, and those that are young enough to possess them will only be able to conjure vague memories of a very unexciting BBC Micro. Unlike other subjects included in the National Curriculum, all of which are very well established, ICT is a newcomer. As any newcomer it is experiencing the trials and tribulations of the 'settling-in' stage. It still has to establish itself, consolidate its role and purpose, and the hardest part, win over the 'old boys' and become an accepted part of the group. As the group includes teachers who have long been known to be greatly affected by their own educational experiences, the process is going to take time. This book aims to win over the 'group' and bring ICT a step closer to full acceptance.

Technicalities

One of the first things that puts many teachers off is the thought of having to deal with technical information they have no desire to master and which they fear they will be unable to master. Luckily, computer technology is such that one of the criteria for advancement is its ability to evolve into a non-technical, more user-friendly device. Teachers no longer have to contend with the dreaded DOS prompt, with its threateningly uninspiring black screen. Instead we have pointers and pictures that allow us to carry out all our work at the click of a button.

One of the aims of this book is to assist teachers in their use of ICT in the learning and teaching process and to go some way in helping them to become technically proficient in an educational context. How technical this should be depends on the role of the teacher concerned. The ICT co-ordinator will need greater proficiency than the non-specialist classroom teacher, and those that are responsible for managing networks will need further expertise still. What is certain is that all teachers will need a rudimentary proficiency to get the best out of the technology they are presented with. For example, whilst it is not essential to know the difference between a JPEG and a clothes peg, there will be times when this knowledge will help a teacher make an informed decision. A JPEG is a good file format for Web graphics (when size matters) because it is a compressed file format that reduces file sizes and critical download times. For high-resolution images however a JPEG is not the best option as some loss of quality takes place during the compression process. Picking out what is useful, relevant and necessary for the primary classroom is always going to be the tricky part. Trainers and publishers will need to meet the challenges here.

The integration model

This book also aims to de-mystify the computer and uncover it for what it is: an educational tool that can enhance the quality of education we provide in schools. Whilst favouring the integration model as a means of delivering ICT, it is also acknowledged that the acquisition of a few basic skills is required to make the model work effectively. Setting time aside for this skills development is crucial for both teachers and pupils. Teachers will need to find appropriate training programs and then physically sit down in front of a computer and play. Pupils too will need to be given time to familiarize themselves with a program and with the help of a teacher who has gone through a similar process this should be a less painful activity.

There will be times however when teaching ICT as a discrete subject will be acceptable and the best way forward. A twenty minute tutorial on the basics of spreadsheet formulae will arm pupils with the necessary knowledge and skills to integrate ICT within, for example, a maths investigation. For the busy primary teacher who has to juggle an over-burdened timetable the integration model, which allows for dual objectives, should be embraced. It is important to note however that for successful integration, teaching and learning objectives for both ICT and the integrated subject should be set out clearly. An amalgamation of fuzzy objectives will benefit neither. For this to be possible teachers will need a thorough understanding of the knowledge and skills encompassed in the National Curriculum (2000) for both ICT and the integrated subject. Teacher training institutions have already begun to meet the challenges and LEAs, schools and teachers will need to do the same.

Organization

This book has been divided into four distinct chapters. The first concentrates on hardware and covers many practical issues that teachers need to be aware of. A technical awareness has been provided for those teachers that are interested and as a point of reference whenever the need may arise.

The second chapter takes a look at software and highlights many legal, technical and practical issues that both classroom teachers and ICT co-ordinators will need to contend with. A section on Microsoft Windows has been included in recognition that this is a common interface used by pupils and teachers at school as well as at home.

The third chapter is a generic look at the main types of applications that will provide coverage of the ICT curriculum at Key Stages 1 and 2.

The final chapter takes a thorough look at the Internet and highlights its role in the educational context.

All chapters follow a common format and provide much more than just the knowledge required for a primary teacher to deliver pupils' statutory entitlement of ICT. The section headings incorporate a combination of practical, technical, and additional information that will more than arm the non-specialist primary teacher. In a world of confusing computer acronyms a glossary has been added that contains a useful list of computer terms to help unpick what is often annoying 'computer-speak'. The resources section at the end of each chapter aims to direct teachers to useful resources that may take the form of books, software, hardware and web addresses. A cautionary note about the latter, however, must inform teachers that the very nature of the Internet and its fluidity may mean that some of the websites indicated may disappear or move without any notice whatsoever. Also, teachers who decide to download files from sites suggested do so at their own risk.

Chapter 1
Hardware

The information in this chapter provides a basic understanding of the hardware available and how it works. Thankfully, with the user-friendly PCs available nowadays, it is not imperative to know about the detailed internal circuitry of your PC, but knowledge of the basic principles involved will not only greatly increase a teacher's confidence but also ensure that key pieces of hardware are operated correctly, maintained efficiently and used effectively. Although computer engineers are continually trying to design ways of cramming more processing power on to smaller and smaller silicon chips, a computer is essentially a machine that only understands two pieces of data, a 1 and a 0. All its capabilities – and its limitations – are based on representing data using combinations of these two building blocks.

So what is 'hardware'?

Hardware comprises all the physical pieces of equipment that make up a computer system: the monitor, keyboard, central processing unit (CPU), mouse and any other peripheral devices such as printers and scanners. Software, which we will look at in the next chapter, is what instructs the computer and makes it perform the functions we want it to do.

The personal computer

A brief history of computers

Charles Babbage is often referred to as the inventor of the first computer. In fact, he never finished his 'analytical engine' and some would argue he would have had problems in doing so owing to the constraints of technology in the 1820s. However, his place in computer history is justified on the grounds that his ideas embodied many of the principles used later in the design of modern computers. The ENIAC (Electronic Numerical Integration And Calculator), built by Presper Eckert and John Maunchly for the US Army in 1945 used valve technology and needed over 70 square metres of floor space. The valves, made out of glass, were extremely heavy, and the need for large amounts of power meant that everything got extremely hot – and very bothered – especially when a valve blew up, which happened more often than they cared to admit.

In fact, the development of the modern computer was thwarted until the valve was replaced by the microchip, which used transistor technology. When this took place in the mid 1960s, the microchip was on the verge of changing everything. Computers became quicker, cheaper and smaller and the microchip revolution was well under way.

In 1977 the very first personal computer was produced by Apple. The company named it 'Apple II' and it was the first computer marketed for the masses that required no knowledge of electronics or computing.

In 1981, keen to retain its position within the business market, International Business Machines (IBM) introduced the IBM PC. It was also the first computer to use a new operating system called MS-DOS.

In 1984, to keep up with IBM, Apple brought out another version of the personal computer – the Macintosh. This was far more user-friendly as it used a Graphical User Interface (GUI). The GUI made it possible to control the computer using a mouse and pictures on screen rather than the cryptic text commands of MS-DOS.

PCs today

Personal computers now come in all shapes and sizes and, at a price, in colours other than grey. The last decade has seen two major changes: the first is the continuing reduction in size and the second, the increase in processing power and capability. Computers have also become relatively cheaper as, for the same cost (or less), you can buy an ever-increasing range of features.

Most computers used at home or at school are usually known as Personal Computers, or PCs. These are named after the original IBM PC that was introduced in 1981, although most PCs are in fact clones of the IBM PC. In other words, they work in the same way as an IBM PC but are not made by IBM. The Apple Macintosh, however, uses a different operating system and until recently could not run the same software. New Apple computers offer a high degree of compatibility with the IBM PC.

The standard PC is a desktop model with a central processing unit (CPU), monitor and keyboard. However, portable PCs are increasingly popular and range from small palmtops to larger laptop models. Notebook or laptop computers increasingly offer the same features as desktops, while weighing on average less than 3kg, but are expensive compared with their desktop counterparts.

Whatever model you choose, a computer will have four essential components:
- a central processing unit (CPU), which can be built-in (as in a portable) or free-standing
- a keyboard through which data or commands are input
- a monitor or screen to display information
- a mouse or pointing device to navigate the screen.

Why you need to know these facts

For teachers to deliver the Programme of Study for information and communications technology, a computer is a necessary resource (though much valuable work can be done without one). A computer is able to extend concentration, increase motivation and develop perseverance in many pupils who may find other methods less stimulating.

Vocabulary

Pentium – name for the processor developed by Intel.
Docking station – required by a notebook to connect to a desktop PC.
Dumb terminal – a computer programmed to carry out one function or task, such as an electronic word processor.
Acronyms
PC – Personal Computer.
CPU – Central Processing Unit.
K (Kilobytes) – the way we measure the size of a computer's memory; these days, memory is likely to be measured in Megabytes and Gigabytes (Mb and Gb).
MHz – measure of how fast a computer's processor can work, in MegaHertz.

Hardware

- The very first personal computers to come on the market were sold in kit form.
- The first IBM PC was launched in 1981 and cost $4300. It offered a built-in loudspeaker that was able to produce no more than a beep and its two floppy disk drives were able to hold only 160K of data each.
- One of the first really useful computers was developed during World War II by Alan Turing to crack Germany's Enigma codes.
- It takes up to 2000 gallons of water to produce one wafer-thin strip of silicon.
- The first 'portable' computer weighed over 11kg!
- Moore's Law, named after Gordon Moore (co-founder of chip manufacturer Intel), states that a PC's computing power will double every 18 months while chip size will halve. Whilst there is a physical restriction on how small a chip can get, the theory is thus far proving fairly accurate.
- Today's modern microchips can deal with more than 1.6 trillion instructions per second.
- A Pentium chip measuring roughly 2.5cm^2 holds over 3 million transistors.

Common misconceptions

Computers make mistakes.
By their very nature, computers are literally unable to make mistakes. They can develop operational problems, but most computer 'errors' are caused by human error at the input stage.

Golden rules

Avoid turning your PC on and off more than necessary (ideally, not more than once in a day) because this produces wear on the hard disk and circuits don't take kindly to power surges. When it is not in use, simply turn the monitor off, so it will be less of a distraction.

Resources

The Usborne Computer Dictionary For Beginners (Usborne)
Usborne Computer Guides – Computers for Beginners (Usborne)
Recycle-IT – an organization that reconditions old PCs for charities and other good causes (tel: 01582 492436, e-mail: recycle-it@cix.co.uk).

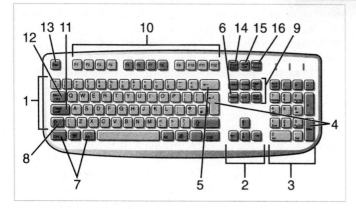

The most common input device on a computer is the QWERTY keyboard. Although the alphabetic keys are similar in appearance to a typewriter, the computer keyboard has many additional keys:

1. The typewriter keys – the middle part of the keyboard resembles the layout of a standard typewriter.

2. Cursor keys – the cursor (or arrow) keys move the cursor so you can navigate around the screen.

3. The numeric keypad – this is useful when you are entering many numbers because of the way the keys are positioned; when NUM LOCK is switched off they can be used as cursor keys.

4. The ENTER/RETURN key – this is used to indicate that a procedure is completed or to enter a line space.

5. The BACKSPACE key – a real life-saver for the non typist, as it deletes the character to the left of the cursor.

6. The delete (DEL) key – this key deletes highlighted text, or the character to the right of the cursor.

7. The control (CTRL) and alternate (ALT) keys – these keys do very little by themselves, but as part of a combination key command they can carry out special procedures.

8. SHIFT – when held down simultaneously with a typewriter key, this produces a capital letter; single capitals should be produced using the SHIFT key.

9. The PGUP, PGDN, HOME and END keys – similar to the cursor keys, these enable the user to find different parts of their document quickly. PGUP and PGDN move the cursor up and down your document one screen at a time. HOME and END move the cursor either to the beginning or end of a line or perhaps the beginning or end of the document, depending upon the program being used.

10. The function keys (F keys) – these perform special functions which vary depending on the software being used.
11. CAPS LOCK – this also produces capital letters, but works like an on/off button and does not need to be held down.
12. The TAB key – this produces indents when typing text.
13. The escape (ESC) key – when all else fails, this key may or may not rescue you (and can also be used to exit from a dialogue box).
14. PRINT SCREEN – this key doesn't actually deliver its promise, but in Windows applications it does transfer your screen image to the clipboard which may then be pasted to another Windows document.
15. SCROLL LOCK – this controls the way in which cursor keys behave in some programs; many programs ignore this key.
16. PAUSE/BREAK – halts a scrolling screen; not widely used.

Why you need to know these facts

The keyboard is the most common input device used with all personal computers. Learning to use it efficiently and effectively will increase productivity.

Amazing facts

● Some of the very first keyboards to be produced were made without any protective cases at all. Computer enthusiasts used to build wooden cases for this purpose.
● When asked to 'Press any key to continue', do not take this literally. The SHIFT, CTRL and ALT keys and the 5 in the middle of the numeric keypad do not work in this situation!
● Have you ever wondered why the arrangement of keys on a standard keyboard is so awkward? When mechanical typewriters were first invented in the 1800s they were large and clumsy, and so to slow typists down and avoid the jamming of keys, the most-used keys were spread out around the edges of the arrangement.
● A more efficient keyboard layout was later designed by August Dvorak in the 1930s. However, despite its more efficient layout the Dvorak keyboard has never grown in popularity, probably because people have been reluctant to re-learn typing skills.
● There is now a keyboard that uses fingerprint recognition technology in order to increase computer security. The scanned fingerprint takes the place of a password but is far more secure as it is unique – and of course you don't need to remember it!

● Never leave drinks close to your keyboard. Sweet drinks are particularly harmful, as when spillages dry they make the keys stick.
● Avoid placing your computer next to a radiator, as it will be more likely to overheat.
● Never plug your keyboard into your computer while it is switched on.

● Most computer manuals have numeric codes for many foreign characters. For example, if you need the French é character, hold down the ALT key and type 0233 on the numeric keypad. When you let go of ALT, the appropriate character will appear (for this to work make sure that NUM LOCK is turned on).
● No matter how hard you try to follow correct procedure, there will be times when you get a complete screen freeze, and the only response you can muster from your keyboard is a rather annoying beep. There is a last resort: pressing the CTRL, ALT and DELETE (not backspace!) keys simultaneously will re-boot your computer. Note, however, that all unsaved work in any applications open before rebooting will be lost.
● Finding highlighting with a mouse a little tricky? Try the keyboard method instead: hold down the SHIFT key and press the right and left arrow keys.

Should infant pupils always work with lower-case keyboards?
This really is up to the class teacher. If the recognition of letters is hindering keyboard entries significantly then a lower-case keyboard may be desirable. A compromise to save purchasing an entirely new keyboard would be to use lower-case stickers on the keys of an existing keyboard which could easily be removed at a later date.

Should primary pupils be taught how to type?
As the use of computers increases, the need to use a keyboard effectively has become more important. Although most children learn to use a keyboard very quickly, they are likely to use only one or two fingers, which limits both speed and accuracy. If you have time (in an after-school club, perhaps), it's worth teaching children how to type properly, and there are a number of software programs which do this.

Hardware

Keyboard Wizard – a portable interactive keyboard that is specifically aimed at teaching basic keyboard skills. Contains 49 pre-programmed tutorials that are ideal for children and teachers alike. Produced by Ablac Learning Works (tel: 01626 332233, e-mail: educ@ablac.co.uk).

Lower case keyboards – many Key Stage 1 teachers prefer to use lower-case keyboards, which are now available at very affordable prices. Available through RM Direct (tel: 01235 826000, www.rm.com).

Ultra Compact Keyboard – a small keyboard which is ideal for users who do not need the number pad. Great for younger children or where space is tight. Available from SEMERC (tel: 0161 827 2527, www.granada-learning.com).

Software

First Keys to Literacy: develops early literacy and keyboard awareness skills simultaneously. Produced by Widgit Software Ltd (tel: 01926 885303, www.widgit.com).

Books

First Steps to Keyboard Skills, Elizabeth Price (Folens): a set of 3 books containing practice exercises that teach typing and keyboard skills.

The mouse

Subject facts

With the almost universal adoption of the GUI, the mouse has become an indispensable input device. It is by far the most popular and widely used pointing device and, with the rise of Microsoft Windows, comes as standard with most computers. Mice vary in shape, size and appearance, from the standard, vaguely rectangular grey device to ergonomically curved ones, not forgetting the mice that look like famous cartoon characters!

The mouse uses a simple 'rolling ball' mechanism. The movements of this ball are picked up by sensors inside the mouse and the messages are sent to the computer with a corresponding movement on screen. Older mice have only two buttons, newer versions have three or four including wheels that are used for scrolling up and down documents. Despite the variety available, nearly all programs will recognize the left button as the one for standard use; this can be changed in Windows Control Panel.

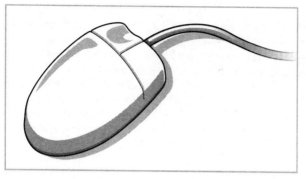

The mouse has five basic applications. You can:
● point to items on screen
● click on items to select them (press the left button once and let go)
● double-click to load a program (two quick clicks)
● highlight text, in order to change font or style, by clicking and selecting the text
● drag items to move them from one place to another (to drag, point to the item, press the left button and, holding it down, move the item to the desired place on screen).
All of these techniques require careful practice.

Whilst the keyboard is probably the most popular input device, the mouse is vital for any computer that uses a GUI. Learning how it works will not only improve its use but should also help to encourage more efficient use and improved upkeep. Teachers of ICT will know only too well how a very expensive computer system can become annoyingly useless when a simple and relatively inexpensive mouse is out of order.

Why you need to know these facts

● Although the mouse was invented in 1964 by Douglas Englebart, the first time it was actually marketed was in 1983 when Apple launched the Lisa computer. IBM's original PC in 1981 did not have a mouse at all as it relied on the keyboard for all data input.
● Did you know there is such a thing as a long-distance mouse? It is normally used on very large screens (at seminars for example) and lets the user point to items on the screen from a distance.
● Technical advancements will mean that very soon mice will be cordless, ball-less and probably integrated into the keyboard.

Amazing facts

● Never use a mouse without a mouse mat. The surface of a mouse mat allows the mouse ball to roll far more smoothly. It is also easier to keep clean which means less dust and dirt entering the mouse ball cavity.
● Avoid the use of temperamental mice which need coaxing. Children will find them very frustrating and the quality of their work will suffer. Everything has a life expectancy and no matter how careful we are, a mouse will eventually need to be replaced.

Handy tips

● The settings on a mouse can be adjusted. If you have Windows, the mouse settings can be changed by accessing the Control Panel. You must remember, however, that the changes will affect all your Windows programs. For left-handed children, the button on the right can be used as the primary button instead of the standard left, while for inexperienced users the speed of the mouse can be reduced, making it less sensitive and therefore easier to control.
● If you find your mouse is starting to stick, remove the mouse ball and, using warm soapy water, give it a wash – remembering to dry it thoroughly afterwards. While doing this, give the mouse ball cavity a quick wipe with a damp cloth and pick out any dirt or fluff that may have accumulated inside. Do not replace the ball until everything is completely dry.
● If the mouse port at the back of your computer does not match the mouse plug, purchase a mouse adaptor. These are available at most computer stores and will prove more cost effective than purchasing a new mouse.
● Keep the balls from broken mice: they can be used to replace balls that go 'walkabouts' in otherwise perfectly good mice.

Resources

Hardware
Infant Mouse – a two-buttoned mouse that is 30 percent smaller than the average mouse; ideal for small children who find a regular mouse difficult to grasp. Available from Research Machines (01235 826000, www.rm.com).
Rollerballs or tracker balls – an alternative to mice, and useful for young children as well as those with poor motor control. Essentially an upturned mouse, the user moves the ball on top to direct the cursor rather than the whole mouse. Available from SEMERC (0161 827 2527) and others.

Peripheral input devices

Although the keyboard and mouse are the most common input devices, there are many other peripheral devices. These include scanners, digital cameras and graphics tablets.

Scanners

Scanners are able to turn 2-D images into digital form so that your computer can reproduce them on screen. Once your image has been turned into a digital file it can be imported into a document or a graphics package that will allow you to manipulate it in a variety of ways.

There are two types of scanner: the flatbed and the hand-held. The latter is the cheaper option, although it tends to produce an inferior image compared with that produced by the flat-bed type, as it relies upon a very steady hand.

Scanners work in a similar way to photocopiers, by homing in on your image and recording which parts are dark and light. Light is bounced off the original image by the scan head (a beam of light), the data is collected by CCDs (charge coupled devices) and converted into digital form by an analogue-to-digital converter in the scanner. Most scanners are able to scan images in colour, monochrome (black and white) and halftone (shades of grey). Colour images are scanned three times by the scan head with the light on each scan being directed through a red, green or blue filter before being combined to recreate the original image.

Digital cameras

Digital cameras, like scanners, turn analogue data into digital form. A photograph is taken as usual but instead of the image being captured on photographic film, it is captured as data so the computer can interpret it. Digital cameras are rapidly falling in price and increasing in quality. They provide a great way of incorporating photographic images into documents – creating personal 'About Myself' books, for example, or recording school trips.

Graphics tablets

In primary schools the mouse is often seen as the obvious drawing tool, but to draw with any real accuracy requires a digitizing tablet, sometimes called a graphics tablet. Quite simply, you draw or write on the surface of the tablet using a special pen and the corresponding image appears on the screen.

Why you need to know these facts

Many ICT projects, particularly multimedia ones, require the use of additional equipment. Scanners and digital cameras are particularly useful when creating multimedia presentations, including web pages for the Internet. They enable you to incorporate photographs and images that would otherwise have been unavailable. By scanning their own drawings or taking digital photographs, even the youngest children can write and illustrate their own stories.

Vocabulary

Acronyms
CCD – Charge Coupled Device.
OCR – Optical Character Recognition.
DIP – Digital Image Processing.
dpi – Dots Per Inch.

Amazing facts

● Most scanners have more than 35 000 CCDs per square centimetre; it would take almost 80 000 CCDs to scan a postage stamp.

Golden rules

● Think carefully before scanning, as scanned images create large files and take up valuable memory.
● Always keep the glass on your flatbed scanner clean as dust particles can affect the quality of images reproduced. Ordinary glass cleaner and a lint-free cloth will do the trick.

Handy tips

● When buying a scanner or digital camera, make sure you also have the appropriate software to run on your computer.
● If scanning pictures which will only be shown on a monitor, a resolution of 72dpi (dots per inch) is enough, as that is the resolution of all monitors. However, if you intend to print images, a resolution of 300dpi is desirable, although not absolutely necessary. You will be limited by such factors as the quality of paper on which you are printing and the maximum resolution of your printer. Remember that the greater the resolution, the larger the file will be, and a single photograph can occupy several megabytes of hard disk space.

● When buying a digital camera, investigate the ease with which images are transferred to the computer. Some cameras make this a very difficult process while others are simple. Cameras that store images straight onto floppy disks are the easiest option.

Scanners often come with OCR software – what is this?
OCR stands for Optical Character Recognition. This enables printed text to be scanned and imported into a word processor. The text is imported as a graphic, the OCR software 'reads' it and converts it to text which you can edit in a word processor. This can save a lot of time and effort as the text does not have to be retyped manually.

Hardware
Kidpen – graphics tablet, from REM (www.r-e-m.co.uk).
Kids Designer Graphics tablet – this comes with software, allowing the pen to be used as a mouse with any program;
Easy Painter Graphics tablet – comes with a two-button stylus. Both are available from SEMERC (0161 827 2527).

The monitor

Types of monitor
The most common type of monitor used is the Cathode Ray Tube (CRT). This is a vacuum tube in which cathode rays produce a luminous image on a fluorescent screen – the same technology as is used in televisions (and which is responsible for its deep shape).

How does a monitor work?
Digital signals concerning the screen image are sent to the video adaptor. Three electron guns located at the narrow end of the CRT (remember the large flat end is the screen) shoot out beams of electrons, one gun for each primary colour (red, green and blue). The beams are passed through holes in a metal plate known as a shadowmask, which aligns the beams accurately. The beams finally hit the screen which is coated with special phosphors. A chemical reaction then takes place, making the phosphors glow. As the chemical reaction only lasts for a fraction of a second,

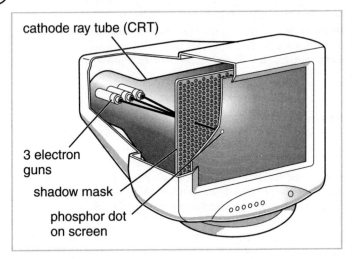

cathode ray tube (CRT)

3 electron guns

shadow mask

phosphor dot on screen

the process has to be repeated many times. This repeat performance is known as the refresh rate, measured in the number of refreshes per second, known as Hertz. Different colours are produced by controlling and combining the intensity of the three electron beams which hit the phosphor dots. These are made up of three primary colours: red, blue and green, which together can make any colour.

Quality
The quality of a screen image is dependent upon its dot pitch (this is a measurement of the distance between dots, or pixels, on a screen) and a monitor's refresh rate. The greater the refresh rate, the better the image. A good monitor has a refresh rate of at least 60Hz.

Alternative screens to CRTs
The alternative technologies to the CRT include the liquid crystal display (LCD) and the TFT (Thin Film Transistor) screen. The LCD screen, found commonly in digital watches and portable computers, produces a fairly poor screen image while a TFT screen produces a good quality image but is still very expensive.

Why you need to know these facts

Once you are a confident user of ICT, you may find yourself spending hours each day staring at a screen, and a poor quality, flickering screen image is not only annoying but also detrimental to your health. A knowledge of resolution and refresh rates is handy when selecting monitors to use in the classroom.

Vocabulary

Refresh rate – the number of times the picture on a screen is redrawn each second.
Resolution – the clarity of a screen image, determined by the number of pixels displayed.
Acronyms
LCD – Liquid Crystal Display.
Hz (Hertz) – the measurement of a monitor's refresh rate.
TFT – Thin Film Transistor.

Amazing facts

● In an area where development of technologies is rapid and the rate of change often exponential, it is perhaps surprising that the technology behind CRT monitors is over 100 years old. CRT technology was developed by Ferdinand Braun in 1897 – though it was not used commercially until the late 1940s.

Golden rules

● Never place disks on top of monitors. You may lose all your data, as monitors produce magnetic fields which may scramble data stored on a floppy disk.

Handy tip

Monitors have come down in price so it is a good idea to invest in the biggest screen possible. This is not only easier to work on, it will also be easier for groups of children to see as they work together or as you demonstrate on screen.

Output devices

Subject facts

Without output devices, using a computer would be a limited exercise. After creating a piece of text, picture or piece of music, you will want to output it – first to the screen, then by printing it, or playing it through speakers.

Printers
The most common form of output device is, of course, the printer. There are three types of printer: the dot matrix, the inkjet and the laser printer.

The dot matrix

The cheapest (and noisiest) of the three, the dot matrix is a common choice for many primary classrooms. It is an impact printer, meaning that it stamps out the image onto the paper, much like a typewriter. Its print head has a vertical row of pins which are pushed out to form the required letter formation. Models with 24 pins produce a higher-quality printout than the cheaper 9-pin versions. Fine for printing text, dot matrix printers are disappointing when it comes to graphics.

The inkjet

Inkjet technology is very different: rather than an image being stamped out by a print head, ink is quite literally squirted onto the page. Instead of a ribbon used by dot matrix printers, the inkjet uses ink cartridges. Inkjets cope easily with both text and graphics, but consumables such as cartridges can be a drain on limited budgets.

The laser

Using technology very similar to that of a photocopier, a laser printer actually prints a page at a time rather than individual characters. A beam of light is used to produce an image on a light-sensitive drum. This image is in turn transferred onto paper, fusing toner onto the page at very high temperatures.

Which is the best option?

A number of factors need to be considered when choosing a suitable printer, not least the cost. Without this restraining factor, laser printers would win hands-down on grounds of quality. However, there are other factors to consider, such as speed, noise, and the balance of initial costs against the costs of consumables such as ribbons, cartridges and toner.

As with any computer purchase it is important to consider the intended use. Is the printer for a classroom where noise is a critical factor or perhaps a computer room where bulk printouts may be useful? Is it for special colour printouts, perhaps for one-off projects such as the school magazine, or for everyday use?

While many schools still use dot matrix printers, the falling price of inkjets has made them an affordable option. For monochrome printing, the laser printer gives the cheapest and best quality printouts per page, but for colour printing, colour laser printers really are out of the reach of most school budgets, for the present at least; colour inkjets can provide excellent quality for reasonable cost.

A printout is the reward for a child's hard work. It also provides evidence of computer work that may be used in a pupil's assessment portfolio, and can often form the basis for a class display. A thorough understanding of printers and the options available is essential when deciding which to buy for the classroom.

Background printing – a feature that allows you to carry on working while a document is printing.
Serial and parallel ports – the connectors at the back of the CPU, which are used to plug in peripheral devices.
USB port – Universal Serial Bus; this is the new standard for connecting peripherals to a computer.
Acronyms
WYSIWYG – this stands for 'What You See Is What You Get' and means that the program can print an exact copy of the screen image.
PPM – speed of printing, measured in Pages Per Minute.

Vocabulary

● When deciding on whose name should appear first, Messrs Hewlett and Packard tossed a coin!
● The desk space taken up by your printer is often referred to as its footprint.

Amazing facts

● You will save printing time and money by opting for 'draft' quality. On most inkjets, even a 'draft' printout is perfectly acceptable.
● Encourage pupils to be sparing in their use of the printer and to make sure they are really satisfied with a piece of work before sending it to print.
● Before printing, use the *Print Preview* facility which will show you what your page looks like before you are committed to printing it.

Golden rules

Will my computer need a USB port if I decide in future to buy a new printer?
Not unless your new printer only supports the Universal Serial Bus (USB) port. Most peripherals have the option to connect to the serial or parallel port – but it is something to watch out for.

Questions

● When buying a printer, make sure that it comes with a cable. More often than not you have to purchase this separately – advice about cabling should be sought when purchasing your printer. Keep a check on prices though, as cables are often cheaper in high street computer stores.

● If using inkjets, make sure the print heads are clean. On the other hand, you must be careful not to use the print head cleaning utility too often as the process wastes ink.

● If it's appropriate, it may be less distracting to save printing until the end of a lesson – or even after it's finished, particularly if you're using a noisy dot matrix printer.

● Inkjets with individual colour cartridges are more cost efficient as each colour can be replaced on an individual basis, as opposed to the whole colour cartridge having to be replaced when perhaps only one of the colours is used up.

● When buying a printer, always get a sample printout on a piece of plain paper. Printouts on specially coated paper are impressive but expensive.

● Keep the printer driver software that comes with your printer safe, as you may need to install this essential software on another computer at some time in the future.

● Always keep at least one spare ribbon or toner cartridge so that you never run out halfway through a print job.

● Print draft printouts on the back of used paper (as long as it is not crumpled).

● Investigate suppliers of recycled printer consumables such as toner cartridges and refill inks for inkjet cartridges.

Special educational needs

Subject facts

The Code of Practice for the Identification and Assessment of Special Educational Needs (DfEE, 1994) specifically emphasizes the role of ICT in special needs education, as does the new National Curriculum (2000). Technologies now exist to enable pupils with a variety of disabilities to access the curriculum.

Children with visual impairment need support at the input stage with the keyboard and at the output stage with the monitor. Larger keyboards with coloured keys to improve contrast can be a big help, while larger screens set at a larger screen resolution help at the output stage.

Speech output, where the computer 'reads' out all text on screen can also be helpful. In the most severe cases, voice input and output may be the only solution.

Children with fine motor control problems (and specifically those that suffer from sudden involuntary movements) can find the mouse an extreme hindrance. However, buying additional hardware when mouse control is a problem may not always be necessary. The first port of call needs to be the Control Panel in Windows, where it is possible to alter the configurations. Changing the speed of the double-click, for example, or the responsiveness of the mouse are both easily done.

Joysticks, overlay keyboards or rollerballs are alternatives, and experimentation will help in finding the right solution for individuals. If problems persist, then try switches – even with one or two switches, the user can control a computer.

The basic idea behind an overlay keyboard is simple. It is a touch-sensitive pad that can be used with paper overlays incorporating text and pictures to input data to the computer. The 'Concept keyboard' is one of the most popular of these and has proved very useful with children with a variety of learning difficulties. They are much easier to control than conventional mice or keyboards and allow the teacher to customize overlays to the needs of children. Complex operations can be simplified and, with the aid of pictures, many language barriers can be overcome too.

Why you need to know these facts

Schools have an obligation to deliver each child's statutory entitlement to the National Curriculum. ICT is able to assist in this process, not only with regard to ICT but all other aspects of the curriculum. Teachers need to be aware of the range of solutions on offer, and whilst financial restrictions will inevitably dictate purchasing decisions, ignorance should never be a contributory factor.

Amazing facts

● Did you know that head-controlled mice are available for those people who do not have the use of their hands?
● One of the UK's first cybercafés for the blind and partially sighted was opened in Preston. Using voice recognition software and screen enlargements, users are able to access the Internet.
● As well as developing alternative keyboard layouts, August Dvorak developed keyboards for use by people with only one hand: one for the left hand, one for the right hand.

Invest in multi-user cabling and interface products that allow at least two devices to be plugged in at a time. A mouse splitter, for example, will allow a standard mouse to be plugged in as well as another alternative input device. As the computer may be used by a variety of children, this saves time and inconvenience.

Resources

ACE Centre Advisory Trust – (tel: 01865 759800, e-mail: info@ace-centre.org.uk). Provides advice, assessment of individual needs and training.

Hardware

Intellikeys – described as an 'intelligent Concept keyboard', this requires no special setting up or programming, is available in a variety of keyboard formats, and automatically recognizes which overlay is in use. Additional overlays can be produced using *Intellitools Overlay Maker*. The latter comes with sample overlays and more than 300 pictures. Both are available from Inclusive Technology Ltd (tel: 01457 819790, www.inclusive.co.uk).

Maltron Expanded Keyboard – works in QWERTY or ABC layout and comes with an integrated steel keyguard and internal switch box. Available from Enabling Computers Supplies (tel: 01785 243111, www.enablingtechnology.net).

Big Keys – a keyboard with 1-inch square keys, simple layout with only ABC, number and arrow keys, available in bright primary colours. No additional software required. Also available are 'Co Pilot' adaptors that allow two keyboards to be connected at the same time; **Keyboard stickers** – available in a range of letter styles and colour contrasts to help children with visual impairment;

Keyguards – these help to avoid unintentional key-presses. Helpful for younger users or children who need to rest their hand on the keyboard. All are available from SEMERC (tel: 0161 827 2527, www.semerc.com).

Concept Universal Plus – concept keyboard designed to enable external fittings to be fitted to a wheelchair;

Concept Plus Multimedia – an updated multimedia version of the Concept Universal Plus. Both available from REM (tel: 01458 253636, www.r-e-m.co.uk).

Magic Touch Screen – this touch screen is great for graphics work, can be used alongside a mouse, and comes with a pen that can be used on screen even when the screen is unattached to the monitor, making it double up as a graphics tablet; **Microsoft Easyball** – ideal for young users, it comes with only one button and can be used alongside a traditional mouse. Both available from Research Machines (tel: 01235 826000, www.rm.com).

Books
Computers and Inclusion: Factors for Success (Becta)

Useful websites
Granada Learning/SEMERC – www.semerc.com.
Inclusive Technology – www.inclusive.co.uk.
Widgit Software – www.widgit.co.uk.
RESOURCE – www.resourcekt.co.uk.
These sites offer information, advice, updates on recent developments together with online catalogues.
ACE Centre – www.ace-centre.org.uk.
Becta – www.becta.org.uk.

Memory and storage

The amount of memory and storage space your computer has is crucial to the way it runs. A computer low on memory will be annoyingly slow and inefficient.

Subject facts

The difference between memory and storage
Although the space on your hard disk is measured in bytes, this is not memory. The hard disk is storage space and its capacity to store is measured in bytes as file sizes are quantified in bytes. In very simplified terms, memory is responsible for the data when your computer is switched on and storage is required to keep your data when the computer is switched off.

RAM and ROM
There are two very important types of memory which require further clarification to facilitate more efficient use of the computer. RAM (Random Access Memory) is the temporary memory required to store the program in use and handle the data it is using. It is responsible for storing the contents of the screen along with the data being transferred to and from any peripherals such as scanners and printers. ROM (Read-Only Memory), on the other hand, holds the basic data your computer needs to start working when it is turned on. This data cannot be changed, hence the term Read-Only.

A Summary

RAM	ROM
Temporary	Permanent
Volatile: loss of power equals loss of data.	Stable: data remains stored, even without power.
Memory that can be read from and written to; therefore data can be changed.	Memory that can be read from but not written to; therefore data cannot be changed.

When a program is loaded it is transferred from the storage area into the memory. When data is later saved it is transferred from the memory to the storage area.

Capacity
The amount of data that can be stored in memory or storage is known as its capacity. Data capacity is measured in bytes.

Bits and bytes
All data storage on a computer is binary. This means that data is represented by combinations of 1s and 0s. A bit is the smallest unit of storage and is either a 1 or a 0. A byte is a group of eight binary bits, and is usually the number of bits required to store one character. This character may be a letter, a number or perhaps a punctuation mark:

01000101	*E*
01010110	*V*
01000101	*E*

The letter E represented in binary. Each 0 or 1 = 1 bit.
8 bits = 1 byte.
 The name EVE therefore requires 3 bytes of storage.

Storage devices
Storage devices have progressed a long way since the days of large magnetic tape. While magnetic storage is still the essential medium for the ever-popular floppy disk, technology has now advanced to the shiny plastic of the CD-ROM (Compact Disc–Read-Only Memory). More recently, the Digital Versatile Disc (DVD-ROM) promises to revolutionize not only computing, but also the entertainment industry.
 At the moment (and moments in computing terms are very short indeed) most schools have two choices when deciding where to store data. Children can either save their

work on the hard disk or to a floppy disk. However, as file sizes increase, alternative storage media providing more space are becoming ever more necessary. High-capacity floppy disks and CDs which are rewritable will become invaluable. Hardware is already meeting these challenges, which is reflected in the increased standard specification of a PC. CD-ROM drives and DVD-ROM drives are becoming standard, although it may take time for these hardware upgrades to become standard in schools. The other alternative, which is becoming more common as primary schools invest in networked computer systems, is to save data on the network server, which will have an area for pupils' work.

The hard disk
The hard disk is an internal storage device that is located inside the computer. Over the years the storage capacity of hard drives has become bigger and bigger and it is now not uncommon to find PCs with hard disk capacities of up to 30Gb and more! The hard disk is actually made up of metal platters coated with magnetic material. Read- and write-heads have the painstaking job of locating data on the platters which are arranged in concentric grooves and organized in clusters.

The floppy disk
Floppy disks are very convenient not only for storing files but also for transferring files from one computer to another. However, the main drawback to the floppy disk is that it cannot store very much data: 720K for a double-sided double-density disk or 1.44Mb (about 1440K) for a high-density disk. With scanned images, a file can instantly become too large for a single floppy disk.

High-capacity disks
As files are getting larger and larger, the development of high-capacity floppy disks is becoming a real necessity. It is now possible to store up to 250Mb of data on a high-capacity disk – that is the equivalent of almost 100 000 pages of text! The disadvantage of these disks is that they require special disk drives, but these are highly portable. Prices of these types of disk and disk drive are coming down as their popularity increases.

The CD-ROM
The CD-ROM is the most popular type of optical disc. Data is written to the disc using powerful laser beams that form pits

(holes) and flats (flat areas). The resulting patterns, which are burned onto the surface, are then read using a less powerful laser beam.

CD-ROMs are able to store up to 650Mb of data. CDs are also no longer read-only; in other words it is possible to make your own CDs using a CD writer (although specialist equipment is required) and use it almost as you would a floppy disk.

The DVD

The next development after the CD has been the Digital Versatile Disc (DVD). In appearance, this resembles a CD, although it is able to hold far more data than its predecessor – up to ten times more, in fact. With this capacity entire movies can be put onto a DVD. Again, a special DVD drive is needed, although these new drives are also able to handle CDs too. Most PCs bought now have a DVD drive as standard.

Understanding file extensions

The three letters after a file's name on a PC can give useful information about the type of file and the sort of data it may contain. This can be very useful when interrogating your files with Windows Explorer. It can help you:

- locate 'lost' files
- delete unnecessary files
- free up valuable memory
- warn you not to touch extremely important files.

File Extension	Type of file	Additional Information
.BAK	Back-up file	Many programs create back-up files without the user realizing. Unnecessary ones could be deleted.
.COM	A command file	A small Windows command file. Never delete a program called command.com, as without it Windows will not run.
.DLL	Dynamic Link Library	This is often a shared program file. Never delete these.
.EXE	Executable file	These are programs. Double-click on these in Explorer and they will run.
.HLP	Help files	Always useful to keep these.
.SYS	System file	Files that control the hardware and software. These are also best left alone.

.TMP	Temporary file	Many programs create temporary files while work on a particular file is being done. They are similar to back-up files, but are usually deleted automatically. Any .tmp files that you do find can be safely deleted.
.WAV	Waveform file	A digital sound file.
.MPG or .MPEG	Motion Pictures Expert Group	A compressed digital audio and video file.
.ZIP	A zipped file	A term used to describe a compressed file. A file that has been 'zipped' (often to save space when transferring files) will need to be 'unzipped' before it can be run.
.HTM or .HTML	HyperText Markup Language	This file extension is used for Web pages.

Common word-processing file extensions

.RTF	Rich Text Format	Can be read by most word-processing programs.
.TXT	Text file	Again, quite a non-specific file type which can be read by most word-processing programs, specifically Notepad and WordPad
.DOC	Microsoft Word file	
.LWP	Lotus Word Pro file	
.WPD	Corel Word Perfect file	

Common spreadsheet file extensions

.123	A Lotus 1-2-3 file
.XLS	A Microsoft Excel file
.LWP	A Lotus Word Pro file
.WPD	A Corel WordPerfect file

Common graphic file extensions

.BMP	A bitmap file	
.GIF	Graphics Interchange Format	A common format found in web pages.

.JPG or .JPEG	Joint Photographic Experts Group	A compressed image. Often, to save space, bitmap images have to be compressed, especially when trying to send a file as an e-mail attachment. JPEG files are one of the best ways of doing this.
.TIF or .TIFF	Tagged Image File Format	Popular format for storing quality images that can be compressed.

Why you need to know these facts

One of the major tasks of managing the class computer is to keep track of all programs and work files. If this management is inefficient it will be difficult to keep up, and very soon your computer will start to slow down and send you messages such as 'insufficient memory'.

The reality of the situation is that over time programs are added and then later deleted, sometimes completely and at other times partially. In times of desperation whole program folders are zapped because no other solution can be found to create enough space for the new program you wish to add. With a little time set aside on a regular basis for a sensible routine space check, life can be made a lot easier.

Furthermore, computers in schools will be used by many, and if everything is saved to the hard disk, space will run out rapidly. But it is not just children's work that vies for disk space. The advent of multimedia has meant that programs are also taking up much more space than before. Managing the hard disk is no longer a job that can be ignored and unless you are lucky enough to be a teacher in a school that is completely networked and has a network manager, at least some time will need to be devoted to disk/file management.

Vocabulary

Back-up – to make a copy of important files on floppy disk or other storage device.
Zip drive – a high-capacity disk drive designed by Iomega.
Cache – a type of memory where frequently used items of data are stored; cache memory is more expensive than normal memory.
Acronyms
RAM – Random Access Memory.
ROM – Read-Only Memory.
CD-ROM – Compact Disc–Read-Only Memory.
CD-R – Compact Disc–Recordable; CD that can be written to once only.

DVD – Digital Versatile Disc.
CD-RW – Compact Disc–ReWritable; A blank CD that can be written to many times.
SIMM – Single In-line Memory Module. These come in two sizes: 30-pin and 72-pin. The 30-pin modules are mainly used by older 386 and 486 processors; the 72-pin modules are used by newer 486 and early Pentium processors.
DIMM – Dual In-line Memory Modules. Used by later Pentiums and all Pentium II and Pentium III processors.
SDRAM – The latest type of DIMM memory module.

Amazing facts

- The root of the Millennium Bug problem of the 1990s was the colossal price of memory in the 1970s. To save on memory, computers were programmed with a two-digit date entry as opposed to a four. Therefore 99 was followed by 00 which computers recognized as 1900, rather than 2000. Had the four-digit 1999 date configuration been used then confusion would have been avoided.
- If you still have a computer running Windows 3.1 you will be restricted to the maximum 8-letter filename. Windows 95 and its successors allow up to 255 characters!
- During the period 1990–9 memory prices fell from £30 per megabyte to £1 per megabyte.
- The Lunar module Eagle, which made its journey to the moon in 1969, had a computer with only 70K of memory.
- A terabyte is equal to some 1 trillion bytes or, to be specific, 1099 511 627 776 bytes!

Common misconceptions

- To say that the values of kilobytes, megabytes and gigabytes are equal to 1000 units is not quite accurate: they are normally rounded off for convenience. In actual fact a kilobyte is 1024 bytes, a megabyte is 1048 576 bytes and a gigabyte is 1073 741 824 bytes, because computers use increasing powers of 2 rather than 10.

Golden rules

- Always buy a PC with as much memory as you can afford.
- Always give files appropriate filenames that will assist when locating them at a later date. This is much easier with programs like Windows 95 which allow longer filenames.
- Never move your computer while the hard disk is in use.
- Never allow children to use disks they have brought from home without checking them first for viruses.
- Likewise, if children are saving work onto floppy disks, make sure these are not taken home.

Handy tips

- Save children's work on floppy disks so as not to occupy valuable space on the hard disk.
- If you do decide to save children's files to the hard disk, group individual's files into folders and sub-folders. For example, you may wish to have a folder for class writing. This folder may in turn contain smaller sub-folders for poetry, non-fiction and so on. This makes files easier to organize and locate.
- Always make back-up copies of important files on floppy disks. If you have many back-ups to make and you have Windows, it is a good idea to use Microsoft *Backup*.
- For Windows 95 and 98 users, two useful programs for disk maintenance are *ScanDisk* and *Disk Defragmenter*. Both will assist in maintaining a healthy hard drive.
- Always remember to empty your recycle bin – though it is useful to give your files a few weeks' grace just to ensure you really do want to get rid of them and that your computer is still working as usual.
- To secure data on a floppy disk, use the write-protect tab. This will prevent new data from being saved to the disk. The write-protect tab can be pulled across the small hole usually found at the bottom left-hand corner of your disk (similar to that on a video cassette). If it is in the write-protect position you cannot save to or re-format your disk.

Questions

Why do two similarly sized Microsoft Word documents vary so much in the amount of memory they take up?
This is possible if the option to *Allow Fast Saves* is enabled. This means that all editing and formatting changes are saved, as well as the document itself. As this occupies a lot of memory, the best action is to disable this function. Find *Options* in the *Tools* menu and click on *Save*; you should now see the *Fast Save* check box, and make sure it is empty. If a document has grown in size in this way, simply *Select All* from the *Edit* menu, cut and paste the entire contents into a new document.

What is fragmentation and why should I defragment my hard disk?
Data is stored on your hard disk in physical locations. After a while your hard disk becomes fairly full and when there is not enough room to store a large file in one place on your disk, out of necessity it is spread around wherever there is space. This will in turn slow down the retrieval of the file as the disk needs to look in more places to find the file.

Fragmentation of many files will eventually slow down the performance of your computer considerably. Defragmenting your disk will tidy up the disk, re-ordering files so that things run more efficiently again.

How much memory should a computer have?
A computer still running Windows 3.1 should be fine with just 16Mb of RAM. However, Windows 95 and above should have a minimum of 32Mb, preferably 64Mb and ideally 128Mb. This may sound like a lot, but software packages are becoming increasingly memory 'greedy'.

Useful websites

Resources

Visit the website of Simply Computers (www.simply.co.uk) to purchase (amongst other things) extra memory modules.

Software
Norton CleanSweep: over time, many odds and ends get stored on the hard drive. With the advent of the Internet and its vast downloads, what once seemed like a reasonably big hard disk shrinks. If you're not sure which files are safe to delete, this piece of software is a must.

Computer networks

Subject facts

Once a school has achieved a ratio of one computer per classroom, the development of a computer network is the next step, so that computers can share software and storage. The physical limitations of classrooms often mean that a separate computer suite has to be set up.

What is a network?
A network is the interconnection of two or more computers. Networks can be divided into Local Area Networks (LANs) or Wide Area Networks (WANs). As the name suggests, a local area network is a smaller network restricted by the physical obstacle of linking computers by cables. A WAN, on the other hand, links computers using telephone wires or radio connections. The network is not therefore restricted to one building and normally covers a wider area.

Are you being served?
The centrepiece of a network is the file server. The file

server is a powerful computer that stores and controls all data on the network. Workstations will access files through the file server. The file server's extensive storage capacity will also mean that it can store all necessary data files.

Network topologies

There are many ways to link computers in a network. Three of the most common are *Bus*, *Token Ring* and *Star*. Below is an example of a Bus network:

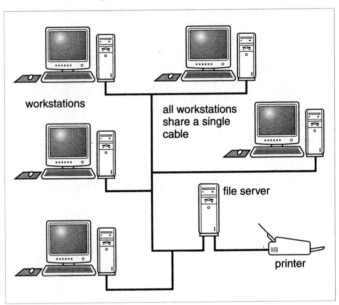

Designing a computer room needs much thought and consideration. Things to consider include:

- size of room
- cabling requirements
- layout of individual workstations
- printing facilities
- work space
- ergonomics
- lighting
- security
- access.

The network: pros and cons

Advantages	Disadvantages
New software need only be loaded once, and can be made available to all workstations.	Needs a trained manager, which may or may not be the ICT co-ordinator.
Peripherals such as printers and scanners can be shared.	A serious problem could affect the whole network.

As workstations do not need a lot of memory (remember the main server stores all data), they are normally cheaper.	Viruses are easily spread across a network.
All administrative tasks can be carried out at the server, saving valuable time.	
CD-ROMs can be accessed by multiple users at one time.	

As schools build up their computing capabilities, their needs will gradually change. When appropriate computer:child ratios are achieved, networking will be the only logical response.

Why you need to know these facts

Node – another name for a computer that is connected to a network, more commonly referred to as a workstation.
Print server – a machine dedicated to controlling print jobs for the network.
Ethernet card – used to connect a PC to a network.
Acronyms
LAN – Local Area Network.
WAN – Wide Area Network.
TAN – Total Area Network.

Vocabulary

● Infra-red technology means that a laptop can communicate with a PC without a cable.
● Whilst cabling is a problem for networking computers today, technology is fast moving towards a wireless future.

Amazing facts

There is no getting away from the technical side of networking. Rather than struggle with all the decision making yourself, seek professional advice. It is better to opt for a professional set-up that will be tested to make sure it works by experts (and may be covered by a maintenance policy) than to try to cobble together an unreliable system that may prove more costly in the long run.

Golden rules

You don't have to be networked to share a printer. If you have computers located in the same room, they can share a printer using a printer switch. These are available from all good suppliers of computer equipment.

Questions

Can laptops be connected to a network?
Yes, but a special network card is needed.

Does the concept of a computer suite go against the models of good practice based on integration?
Very often a computer suite is the only practicable solution to a school's ICT strategy. In primary schools, where classroom teachers are responsible for delivering the whole curriculum, the computer suite becomes a necessary tool and a facilitator to learning and communicating. It has failed its role if it is used solely to teach ICT skills out of context. The way a computer suite is used is largely governed by the school's schemes of work and how these interact with the overall curriculum and ICT policy.

What is the difference between a peer-to-peer network and a client/server network?
In a peer-to-peer network configuration, each computer on the network is equal with each other. There is no file server and computers simply share files and resources. A client/server configuration has a central server which is powerful enough to provide all workstations with the services they need. The latter is a far more secure network.

What is an intranet?
An intranet is a closed network that uses the same protocols (rules and standards of communication) as the Internet. You can download a whole website, for example, and store it on an intranet so that pupils can access it offline (that is, without running up a telephone bill at the same time).

Resources

Class Link Network – a class networking solution for schools provided by Viglen (tel: 020 8758 7027, e-mail: schools@viglen.co.uk).

Books
Connecting Schools, Networking People 2000 (Becta).

Maintenance

From time to time a hardware problem will need the attention of a professional engineer. It is always worth investing in a maintenance contract with a reputable company. Advice can be taken from LEAs and a variety of regional ICT centres. Larger computer suppliers such as Research Machines have their own maintenance departments, which are well worth investigating. While budgets may be stretched, not investing in a maintenance contract may be a false economy. A relatively simple fault may render a £1200 computer system useless, and calling engineers for individual repairs on an ad hoc basis will normally prove far too expensive.

Dealing with faults

A clear, simple and effective system of reporting faults needs to be established throughout the whole school. Simply stating that a computer does not work will not be an acceptable response to service engineers when faults are reported. Staff will need to detail the exact fault, give details of equipment and relevant serial numbers. They will also need to note any error messages and carry out basic checks: for example, if the printer is not working, has it been switched on? Is it online? Has it enough paper?

Cleaning

There is no doubt that primary classrooms provide a real challenge when trying to keep the classroom computer clean. The cleaning of computers is not, however, purely for aesthetic reasons. Keeping a computer clean and free from harmful substances will not only extend its life but is also vital for the safety of children and staff. Nursery and infant classrooms in particular tend to contain many different potentially harmful substances, such as water, glue and sand. Always try to locate the computer well away from such hazards. Remember that the computer is an electrical device and that all the normal safety precautions need to be adhered to – splashes of water, paint or soft drinks need to be avoided at all costs. If they do occur, switch the computer off at the mains and if it is a minor spill, allow to dry, or call an engineer to have a closer look. Sticky fingers are another common problem and children need to be encouraged to wash and dry their hands before working at the computer. Plastic overlays that protect keyboards when in use are available, and dust covers and keyboard pockets are useful at the end of the school day to reduce the need to dust your computer. Special screen wipes to keep monitors clean are also available, but any standard glass cleaner will do.

Location

With limited space available in the classroom, locating the classroom computer can be difficult. If there is only one suitable electrical socket, the decision is almost taken out of your hands. However, a few factors need to be considered:

● avoid placing the computer near any water/sink areas
● avoid places which allow direct sunlight on to the screen
● avoid placing a computer close to a thoroughfare where passers-by may be tempted to touch
● to avoid distractions, place the computer where children are not able to look at the screen when they are not working on it.

Why you need to know these facts

It is vital that all classroom teachers are aware of the potential hazards that may befall the classroom computer and that the necessary precautions are taken. Indeed, it is a statutory requirement clearly stated in the National Curriculum (2000). With a sensible routine the classroom computer can be well looked after and provide reliable service for many years.

Amazing facts

● There is a school of thought that advocates never switching off a computer, even at the end of the day, because frequent restarting of a machine gradually wears out its hard disk. Surges of electricity can be damaging to circuits, though computers today are much more resilient.
● Did you know that there are specially designed vacuum cleaners for keeping keyboards free of dust?

Golden rules

● As with any other electrical equipment, never allow very young children near power sockets.
● Never place a computer near water, paint, glue or sand, which could find their way in to the computer and reduce its lifespan.
● Ensure cabling is not a tripping hazard. Extension cables are widely available and inexpensive. If cable does need to run across the floor, it should be protected with rubber matting.
● Always use dust covers when the computer is out of use for long periods.

- Label the cables at the back of your computer so they are easily identified when the need arises to reconnect them.
- Buy cable tubes to stop the tangled 'spaghetti junction' look at the back of the computer (which is unattractive, confusing and dangerous).
- To avoid younger children inserting objects into the floppy disk drive (a favourite trick!), cover it using a piece of stiff card and sticky tape.
- A small, soft-bristled paintbrush or make-up brush is ideal for gently cleaning between the keys on a keyboard. Always make sure the computer is turned off first!
- Appoint children as computer monitors and train them to look after the computer.

Ask the class to design a poster about the do's and don'ts of computer usage. Display these around the computer area.

Keyboard skins – clear covers that protect your keyboard from dust and liquid spills. These can be left on during typing with no interference. Available from SEMERC (tel: 0161 827 2527, www.semerc.com).

Health and safety

Computers in schools, perhaps more so than computers in other working environments, carry with them many health and safety issues. These issues are paramount when organizing computers in the classroom.

Setting up the computer

It is very important that a computer is set up appropriately for children. The computer needs to be placed on a surface that is of an appropriate height and away from sources of glare (anti-glare filters are a sensible precaution). The monitor should ideally be a fraction below eye-level. Monitors placed too high are often the cause of neck and eye strain. Children should sit an arm's length away from the monitor and their arms should roughly form a right angle as they type on the keyboard. Children typing for any length of time should be given wrist pads which enable the wrist to rest at a comfortable angle.

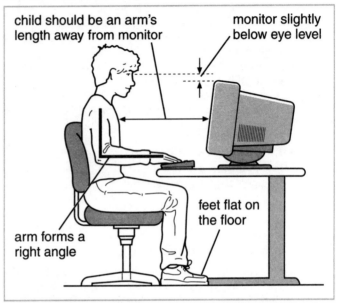

child should be an arm's length away from monitor

monitor slightly below eye level

arm forms a right angle

feet flat on the floor

Chairs should be appropriately sized: children need to be able to put both feet firmly on the floor and should never dangle their feet. Adjustable chairs are a good (but expensive) option.

Time at the computer

Getting interested children to finish their work on time is sometimes difficult. However, children should never be expected to sit at a computer for more than 30 minutes at a time. A few short breaks are far better than longer breaks followed by long periods of sustained computer work.

Equipment

The computer is, first and foremost, an electrical device. Therefore all the usual safety precautions pertaining to electrical equipment should also apply to your computer. Like all other pieces of electrical equipment, computers should undergo annual checks by qualified electricians. In the classroom, children should be made aware of the rules pertaining to the safety of the computer, and these should be reinforced at all possible opportunities.

With computers playing a greater role in all primary classrooms, teachers have a responsibility to make them as safe as possible to use. With very young children, potential problems tend to be involved with the dangers associated with any type of electrical equipment. As children get older and their allocation of computer time increases, problems of prolonged repetitive tasks become the focus of concern. Any activity which is carried out for long periods of time will prove damaging in the long run. The effects of the debilitating condition of RSI (Repetitive Strain Injury) have been well documented, and whilst a lack of funds often minimizes the risk of prolonged sessions at the computer, good practice should always be followed. Children need to be made aware of the very real health risks that poor computer use can cause. Health and safety features should be budgeted for and not be left to chance.

● Did you know that modern light-touch keyboards are believed to be more likely to cause RSI than old-fashioned hard hitting typewriters?
● A few simple eye exercises can help to maintain concentration when working at a monitor for sustained periods of time. Focus upon objects at a distance and then something that is close up. To remind you to give your eyes a rest, you can download the *Eyesaver* program available from Dolland & Aitchison's website (www.dollond.co.uk).

● Buy symmetrical mice as the ergonomically shaped ones are less favourable for left-handers.
● If illumination is a problem, try spot lamps. These are often a lot better than just using overhead lights.
● When buying tables or desks for computers, buy ones with adjustable height capabilities.

● Ask pupils to create posters based on health and safety issues concerning the use of the classroom computer. These could then be displayed around the computer.
● When children are new to computers or to a particular piece of software, it's helpful to create a 'crib sheet' with simple instructions and solutions to common problems.
● Children can be good peer tutors: if they are working in small groups at the computer, ask each group to pass on instructions to the next group as they hand over.

Hardware

Microsoft Natural Keyboard – an ergonomic keyboard designed with a built-in palm rest; **The Smart Keyboard** – a keyboard made out of durable rubber that you can even roll up! The nearest thing to an indestructible keyboard, but not suitable for prolonged typing and a fairly expensive option. Available from most high street suppliers of computer equipment.

SIS Wide Workstation – a height-adjustable workstation, available from many suppliers of office/school furniture.

Security

Subject facts

As computer crime has increased, so market forces have responded to the need for computer security. Computer hardware will for any school form a significant budgetary commitment. Investing in its security is therefore a very sensible option.

Frames

Unlike cabinets (see below), where the whole computer is encased when not in use, frames are used to 'capture' the equipment, making removal difficult. Most systems allow for occasional easy removal by a key holder.

Steel cabling

The use of steel cables is another popular method and relies on anchoring the equipment to a secure surface using steel plates and cables.

Secure cabinets

Secure cabinets are built to provide a total lock-up for a computer workstation. They tend to take up far more room than frames, though, and are an expensive option.

Marking

There are many reasons for marking your hardware. Firstly, any stolen items recovered by the police can be identified immediately. Secondly, marking turns your computer into a less marketable item. While professional marking systems are good, perhaps the best deterrent would be to mark, say, the underside of your equipment in a bold colour using acrylic paint so no one would want it anyway. Don't get too carried away with painting marks on the PC: a postcode and a couple of initials will suffice!

Insurance

Insurance can be a costly affair. Surprisingly, many schools still opt not to insure ICT equipment, although any simple cost–benefit analysis fails to justify this strategy. If budgetary cuts need to be made then the decision should not be *whether* to insure or not but *what* to insure. To reduce costs, omit cheaper items such as older dot matrix printers or other peripherals which are generally cheaper to replace than an entire multimedia machine.

Computer crime inflicted on schools is an ever-growing problem. Schools are now purchasing industry-standard machines and these are a viable commodity for any thief. Schools need to make sensible decisions not only about preventative measures but also about damage-limitation strategies. Ignoring them may not only be a false economy but could be detrimental to the education of many children.

Why you need to know these facts

- Did you know that there are security systems that will page owners of an illegal movement of their equipment?
- It is possible to purchase motion alarms, which detect illegal movements and sound an alarm when activated.

Amazing facts

- Note down the serial numbers of all your ICT equipment, remembering to include peripherals, and note also the location of each computer so if a machine does go missing it can be identified immediately.
- Clearly mark all equipment with the name and postcode of your school. Put up warnings that may deter thieves.
- Lock classroom/computer room doors when not in use.
- If cost is a determining factor when insuring ICT equipment, prioritize rather than not insuring at all.

Golden rules

Carlan Computer Security – (tel: 024 7635 6266).
MCS – (tel: 020 8502 0905).
SELECTAMARK Security Systems plc (tel: 0800 163295).

Resources

Chapter 2
Software

Once you have your hardware set up (or have plucked up the courage to use it!), what are you going to use it for? The purpose of using a computer is to fulfil a task, after all, so you need to select software which is appropriate. There are two types of software: *applications* (programs that provide a framework which you fill), and those that are *reference* programs.

Applications

These programs are also known as *generic* software because although you can buy different titles, they will all perform similar functions. They often come with your computer when you purchase it and may include the following:
● Word processing software, for creating text – anything from a shopping list or a brief letter to an entire book.
● Spreadsheets, for working out mathematics (your school budget, for example) or for modelling situations (such as running the tuck shop).
● Databases, for storing and analysing information – anything from pupils' names and addresses to a project on who lived in their street 100 years ago.
● Desktop publishing programs, for designing posters, school newsletters or even the school prospectus.
● Drawing and painting programs, which enable even the youngest children to experiment with colour and shape.

Reference software

This is software which you purchase (usually on CD-ROM nowadays) because it contains material that you want. Much of it is multimedia – that is, it contains pictures, sounds and animations as well as text. It includes the following:

- encyclopaedias, dictionaries and other reference works
- talking stories
- subject-specific software – to practise sequencing, for example, or to compose short tunes in music
- Clip Art or extra fonts for your computer
- extra utilities such as anti-virus software or software to connect to the Internet.

Educational software has become one of the biggest growth areas within the educational publishing sector for some years. Multimedia has given software greater life and vitality; software can now be interactive, make sounds, and provide dimensions that pupils of today demand and respond to. This chapter looks at the range of software available for primary schools.

Software issues

What is software?

If hardware is made up of all the physical parts of the computer, software consists of the instructional programs that tell the computer what to do and how to do it. Software is written in the form of programs which are made up of very precise instructions.

The language of computer programming

If a program is a set of instructions for the computer, it is logical to assume that they must be written in a language that can be understood by the computer. Computers understand binary code, often referred to as machine code. However, writing programs in this language is painstakingly slow. To help programmers to write computer software, special programming languages have been developed.

Common programming languages include BASIC, COBOL, PASCAL and C++. In fact, even Logo, developed by Professor Seymour Papert and used widely in schools, is also a simple programming language. Once a program has been written in a computer language, it has to be translated using a special program called a compiler.

The operating system

When you buy a computer it usually has an operating system already installed. An operating system is made up of all the instructions and utilities software required to make the computer function – the operating system is in control of every part of your computer. Most computers in schools run an operating system called MS-DOS. As this is a text-based system, Graphical User Interfaces (or GUIs) such as Microsoft Windows (see page 55) are run on top of MS-DOS. They work together and are responsible for the smooth running of your computer.

Licensing issues

Software is subject to the same copyright laws as literary works. Thus the Copyright, Designs and Patents Act of 1988 applies to a piece of software just as it does to a novel or piece of non-fiction.

When software is bought there is normally an agreement entered into between the user and the manufacturer regarding its usage. Unless a multiple-user licence is bought, a program may only be installed on to one machine. If you wish to install the same program on another machine, you either have to remove the program from the first machine or purchase a multiple-user licence. These vary from a licence covering a specific number of machines to site licences, which are normally based upon the size of the school. Most suppliers will allow schools to upgrade to a site licence at a later date. Whilst there is a charge to upgrade your licence, it is more cost effective than purchasing another copy of the program.

Viruses

Viruses are a potential hazard for any computer user. In very simple terms, they are malicious programs aimed to cause systematic harm or havoc. The most common ways in which computers are infected by viruses are via e-mail attachments, files downloaded from the Internet or files contained on contaminated floppy disks.

The only solution to viruses is to purchase (and use) anti-virus software. This will probably come on a CD-ROM and can be kept up to date by downloading new versions from the supplier's website on the Internet. The following table describes the most common types of computer virus. Most viruses fall into one of these categories, though it should be noted that viruses are being developed all the time and the best strategy to take is to keep your anti-virus software up to date.

Type of virus	Description
Trojan	Virus that 'invades' a computer under false pretences, usually pretending to be a safe program
Logic bomb	Virus that is activated when a particular program is run
Time bomb	Virus that is activated on a particular time and date
Worm	Virus that reproduces itself

Possibly the most insidious of these is the worm virus. Each reproduction goes on to reproduce still more copies of the virus and so this goes on. The exponential nature of the increased volume means that entire networks can be brought down in a very short space of time.

When Microsoft incorporated the ability to write macros (simple programs) in its Office suite it actually provided a tool that could be put to destructive use. These 'macro viruses' are now the most common types of virus.

Precautions
Avoiding the potential hazards of e-mail attachments, Internet downloads and suspect floppy disks means undertaking precautionary measures:
● Never allow pupils to take floppy disks home or bring floppy disks to school unless you have up to date anti-virus software not only on your computer but also switched on. As it takes a little while for the computer to scan every disk that is put in, it can be tempting to turn the anti-virus software off – a temptation you must resist!
● Only download files from the Internet if the site is credible and clearly states that its files are virus-free.
● If in doubt, save files to a floppy disk and then run a virus check on the disk before using it.
● Be wary of files that have an .exe extension. These are executable files that will run if you double-click on them in Windows Explorer. If in doubt, leave well alone.

An exercise in damage limitation
No matter how stringent your precautions are, really determined viruses can still infect systems. In such circumstances, action should be swift. Pupils and teachers must know exactly what to do when a virus is discovered:
● Alert the person in charge of the computers; the ICT co-ordinator, headteacher or the network manager/technician.

● Do not open further files, folders or programs.
● If working on a network, alert all workstations.

The extent of the damage to the computer or work files is dependent on the type of virus unleashed. Some viruses are relatively harmless while others can cause serious damage. The only way to remove the virus is to use a proprietary anti-virus program, remembering that it is likely that some work will be lost, whether saved or not.

Why you need to know these facts

There are practical, educational and legal implications when purchasing new software. The person responsible for co-ordinating this task needs to be aware of all the issues relating to these areas, and anyone responsible for purchasing software needs to think about the most cost-effective way to purchase software titles. How many machines will the software be loaded on to, and is this likely to increase in the future? Is a site licence the best option, and if this is difficult to finance straight away, can it be budgeted for in the future? Once software has been purchased, a few necessary chores need to be dealt with almost immediately. Most suppliers offer a registration service and it is certainly worth taking up, as technical support may depend on it. Licence agreements need to be filed for future reference and if there are any problems pertaining to copyright issues, ICT co-ordinators will need to note that they will be held responsible.

Once software has been installed onto the relevant machines, a period of familiarization is needed, first by the class teacher and then by pupils. As the central role of ICT in schools is focused on integration, the purchasing of software titles is fast becoming a responsibility of many individuals, not just the ICT co-ordinator. A more long-term strategy to buying that is closely linked with the curriculum is certainly preferable to ad hoc purchases. Technical support for non-specialist staff may be needed.

Vocabulary

Beta – new version of software that is still being tested.
Programming – writing computer programs.
Bug – an error in a program's code.
Debugging – correcting errors in a program's code.
UNIX – an alternative operating system to MS-DOS.
Algorithm – a prepared piece of code that is used frequently. Most programmers have a selection of algorithms that can be used instead of rewriting time-consuming code from scratch.

Bundled software – software that comes with the purchase of a new computer. Often called OEM (Original Equipment Manufacturer) software.

Windows CE – a cut-down version of Microsoft's Windows operating system used by hand-held computers.

Driver – software that communicates between the computer and a peripheral device such as a printer.

Acronyms

MS-DOS – MicroSoft–Disk Operating System.

BASIC – Beginner's All-purpose Symbolic Instruction Code

COBOL – COmmon Business Orientated Language.

Amazing facts

● Microsoft's Windows 98 operating system contains over 8 million lines of code!

● The UK government spent a staggering £25 billion to prepare for the millennium (or Y2K) bug. This figure was more per head than any other nation, including the USA, but did prevent the catastrophes predicted by some.

● The most common way a virus might infect a computer is by 'hiding' in a Word document. Once the document is opened, the virus is set free to infect.

● On March 6th 1992, exactly 517 years since the Italian painter Michelangelo was born, a malicious virus named 'Michelangelo' attacked computers all across the globe, turning data into complete gobbledegook.

● Programs are normally encrypted to stop people copying or illegally taking program code.

Common misconceptions

Opening an attachment and not simply the e-mail is the only way a virus can infect your computer.
This used to be the case. Unfortunately a virus named 'Bubbleboy' proved this to be outdated. It was able to infect the computer by the recipient only having to open their e-mail. Luckily the virus proved to be a non-malicious one and only affected users of Microsoft Outlook. Its existence, though, does not bode well for the future where malicious variants will undoubtedly develop. Whilst software developers are continually closing loopholes in their software exposed by viruses, those that write viruses are often one step ahead, and constantly find new ways of writing viruses. Vigilance is the key.

Joke virus alerts are harmless.
At the very least a hoax virus alert takes up valuable time, effort and bandwidth.

What is the difference between freeware and shareware?
Freeware is yours to use and keep for as long as you like,
whereas shareware is used on the understanding that if the
user is satisfied with the product and wishes to keep it after
a set time, a fee must be paid.

***How do I know if my computer has been infected with a
virus?***
Sometimes it will be more than obvious, as a message will
appear on the screen telling you! However, you will often
only be given obscure signs that something is not quite
right. Tell-tale signs include: frequent program crashes for
no obvious reason, missing files, peripherals that suddenly
stop working, slower response times and generally
unexplained irregularities. (Bear in mind, of course, that all
of these tell-tale signs may have alternative explanations,
making confirmation of a virus difficult.)

Handy tips

● Before purchasing new software, check its minimum
system requirements.
● Newer versions of programs now come with small
'uninstall' programs that make removing a program
extremely easy. Use these to uninstall the software and the
danger of accidentally removing a vital file is negligible.
● Check anti-virus disks provided for the administration
computers in schools. These are normally updated every
month and can be used on curriculum computers too.

Golden rules

● Always purchase anti-virus software. Note that Windows
95 does not have any already installed.
● Always complete and return registration forms for new
programs. This will confirm your purchase, permit you to
use any customer care service that may be on offer and
keep you informed of future updates.
● Make back-up disks of programs that allow you to do this.
Keep the master disk in a safe place.

Resources

Useful websites
www.shareware.com – download shareware programs from
the Internet.
www.softseek.com – another site that tracks down free
programs to download.
www.drsolomon.com – a good site to keep you up to date

with developments concerning viruses. Why not sign up to
the free virus alert mailing list?
www.gerlitz.com/virushoax – general advice about viruses
and a descriptive list of virus hoaxes.

Windows

MS-DOS – still around in the background

The success of the home PC has been made possible by the
development of the graphical user interface (or GUI). The
most popular of these is Microsoft's Windows. Before the
popularization of Windows, users communicated with their
computers using text command codes. For the non-
computer expert, DOS commands proved unpopular and
complicated. To make computers more 'user friendly'
Microsoft developed Windows which worked alongside
DOS, providing an interface that negated the need to input
DOS command codes. With this development, computers
were ready for the masses.

The GUI system

The graphical user interface (GUI) is basically a system
designed to control a computer using graphical
representations, referred to as icons. Instead of typing in a
command code, the user simply points to the icon with a
pointing device such as a mouse, and selects it using a
cursor. This in turn initiates the necessary steps for the task
to be completed. Since a GUI bypasses the need for any
specific technical knowledge, it is often assigned the label
'user friendly'.

Versions

The first effective version of Windows developed by
Microsoft was version 3.0, released in 1990, and soon
followed by the increased capabilities of versions 3.1 and
3.11. The Windows platform was given a complete overhaul
in 1995 with the launch of Windows 95 – which was further
upgraded in 1998.

The latest versions, Windows 2000 and Windows
Millennium Edition, are a further attempt to make the PC as
user-friendly as possible and is reinforcing the concept of
the PC as being the central part of the home or workplace.
Icons are based around tasks rather than applications so
access is even more direct.

Windows – a familiar concept

The user-friendly status of Windows has been achieved through the use of familiar terms and concepts. The Windows 'desktop' is a graphical representation of a real desk. Familiar desktop items have been included such as the calculator, notepad, clock, recycle bin (waste-paper basket!) and drawing tools. Individual documents are referred to as files and are stored together in folders and sub-folders. Windows allows the non-technical user to carry out tasks electronically using very familiar concepts.

Desktop security at school

In the school context, the Windows desktop needs some form of security in order to prevent children from changing settings, deleting items, adding software without permission and generally having a free reign over the system. Many software solutions are available. Most deny access to the Control Panel and Windows Explorer, where most damage can be done. Teachers can also set up their own program boxes deciding which programs to allow pupils access to.

The anatomy of a window

Programs running under Windows have a number of standard features:

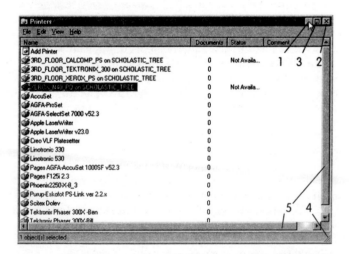

1. Minimize: clicking here reduces the window to an icon at the bottom of the screen. Your program will still be running, but this is a way for you to clear your workspace if the need arises. To return to the original size and position, click on the icon at the bottom of the screen again.

2. Close: when you have finished working with your program you can close the window and stop the program by clicking here.

3. Maximize: if you wish to increase the size of your window so that it covers all of the screen, click on the Maximize button.

4. Resize: to resize your window, position your pointer over the border. The pointer should now change to a double-headed arrow. Now click and hold the mouse button and drag the border to where you wish it to be. When satisfied, release the mouse button.

5. Scroll: there are times when a window cannot display all its contents. In this case you would need to scroll vertically and/or horizontally to view hidden parts of your window.

Drop-down menus

Windows uses a system based on menus for users to make choices about options available to them. Whatever piece of software you are using, there will be a menu bar across the top of the screen with the names of all the menus on offer. A single click on the menu title and the menu will 'drop down', revealing a list of choices and preferences. With practice, it is easy to find the option you are looking for as Windows incorporates a good deal of uniformity. For instance, the *Print* option will always appear in the *File* menu whichever Windows program you are working with. Most Windows programs have a standard set of menus: *File, Edit, View, Window* and *Help*, as well as others more specific to each program. The best way to discover what they all offer is to create a document and try out the changes – you can nearly always undo an option by going to *Undo* in the *Edit* menu.

Finding the right option

Several conventions are used in drop-down menus which you will soon get used to. Three dots after an option indicate that more choices are available; these will be offered using a dialogue box. A tick next to a box indicates that an option is switched on; you can turn it off by clicking with the mouse. A small arrow to the right of an option indicates that another drop-down menu will follow if you point at the option. A single large dot indicates that a selection has been made.

You may find that some of the options in a drop-down menu are grey in colour. This means either that this option is not available with the software you are using, or that you need to select a file or highlight text first.

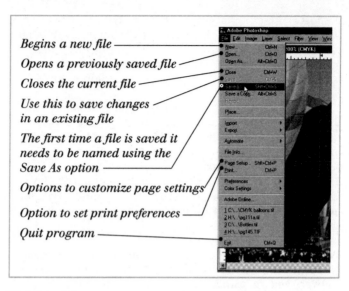

Begins a new file

Opens a previously saved file

Closes the current file

Use this to save changes in an existing file

The first time a file is saved it needs to be named using the Save As option

Options to customize page settings

Option to set print preferences

Quit program

Multi-tasking

One of the great advantages of Windows is that it allows the user to work with more than one application at a time. For example, this means a print job can be started and left to run in the background while you simultaneously move on to some word processing.

Object embedding

If you would like to place a sound or graphic file into a document, the best option is to embed it. To do this you will need to:

- open the file you wish the object to be placed into
- select *Object* from the *Insert* menu
- locate your file from the *Browse* dialogue box.

To make changes to your inserted object, double-click on the object within your document. This takes you to the object's source program where you can edit the object.

Object linking

Object linking is similar to embedding in that it inserts an object into another document. However, when an object is linked, changes made to the object in its source program are automatically updated in the destination document. To link an object, select *Link* from the *Insert* menu as above.

The clipboard

The clipboard is an extremely useful tool for Windows users. Whenever an item is cut or copied, it is sent to the clipboard, which stores it until the item is pasted to a different location. In this way a picture may be cut from Paint and pasted into a Word document with relative ease. However, it should be noted that the clipboard will only store one item at a time and whenever something is cut or copied it will replace the previous item stored on the clipboard.

The spike facility

In Microsoft Word, the spike facility is useful if you need to move several parts of non-adjacent text. Unlike the clipboard, the spike can be added to repeatedly. To do this, simply highlight the item and press CTRL+F3. This may be done as many times as is required. To position the items back on the page, place the cursor in the correct place and press CTRL+SHIFT+F3.

Files and folders

When a piece of work has been completed it is saved as a file. A group of files can be saved together in a folder. A folder may in turn contain several sub-folders, containing different groups of files.

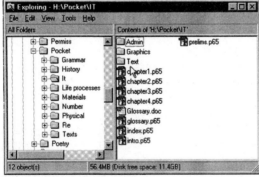

Organizing files

Information can only prove useful if it is efficiently organized so that access can be gained quickly and with ease. Learning to organize files on a computer is an essential skill and will pay dividends as files and folders begin to increase in size.

A busy classroom computer can quickly accumulate many files and become disorganized. For the inexperienced user the tendency is to save files to the hard disk using the default settings on offer. Unfortunately, if you do this for a whole year, all the files will be kept in the same location and finding any one particular file will take longer and longer. It would be like putting a year's worth of writing in one box with no added organization. It's far more efficient to create several folders and label them so that finding particular pieces of work is much easier. Windows allows for this type of organization electronically and has made life easier by using familiar terms such as files and folders.

Most users develop their own filing system over time. Possibilities include organizing folders in date order, with work filed in half-termly batches, or subject-based, where science, history, geography and so on would be stored separately, or even group-based so that the red group would always have its work saved in a folder labelled 'red group'.

But it need not stop there, these folders could then be subdivided further.

The example below shows how work can be sensibly grouped into folders.

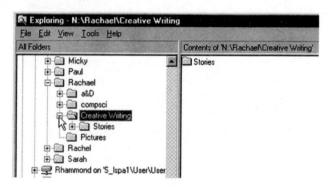

The diagram above shows a hard disk with two main folders called 'Pictures' and 'Creative Writing'. The Creative Writing folder has a further sub-folder called 'Stories'. The minus sign next to the Creative Writing folder shows that the folder has sub-folders which are listed (underneath). The plus sign next to the sub-folder Stories means that there are sub-folders within this folder too, but these are not yet shown. To list a folder's sub-folders, click once on the plus sign. To open a folder and see its contents (files and sub-folders), double-click the folder icon.

Creating a new folder

- Open Windows Explorer.
- Click on the C: drive icon.
- Select *New* from the *File* menu and choose *Folder.*
- A new folder icon will appear in the right of the window.
- Name your folder by placing your cursor in the box next to your folder icon and typing the name of your choice.

Creating a sub-folder

● Still in Explorer, select the folder you just created.
● Select *New* from the *File* menu and choose *Folder*.
● A new folder will appear on the right-hand side of the window which is within the folder you just created.
● Name your folder by placing your cursor into the box next to your folder icon and typing the name of your choice.

Investigating files and folders

There are two ways of exploring files and folders: Windows Explorer and My Computer. Both allow you to search a chosen location and make amendments and changes to folders. Which one you use is a matter of personal preference.

Deleting files

Whole folders may be deleted simply by selecting the appropriate folder and selecting *Delete* from the *File* menu. If only selected files need to be deleted, then open the folder, select the file and delete in the same way. Remember that the Recycle Bin will allow you to rescue files and folders you may wish to restore after deleting.

Copying files

There may be times when a particular file needs to be copied to a different location. This may be onto a floppy disk which can then be used to transfer the file to another computer or it may simply be to another folder. Copying files is a very easy procedure:
● Make sure the file you wish to copy and the location you wish to copy it to are both visible in Windows Explorer.
● Using the right button on your mouse, click on the file you wish to copy.
● From the menu that appears select *Copy*.
● Right-click on the folder you wish your file to be copied to, or the A: drive to copy to a floppy disk.
● From the menu that appears, select *Paste*.

Getting to grips with the software that controls your computer empowers the user, making their use of the computer more organized, efficient and productive. Windows in particular comes with many extra programs and some of them are designed to make life a lot easier. Once you have become familiar with using your computer, it's worth spending time looking more closely at its manuals and online tutorials.

Why you need to know these facts

Software

Amazing facts

● Co-founder of Microsoft Bill Gates was a billionaire by the age of 30 thanks to the development of MS-DOS.
● With the advent of Windows 95 you are no longer restricted to an eight-character filename. You may now have up to 255 characters!

Vocabulary

Desktop – the digital version of a desk where icons for files, folders and programs can be arranged.
Icon – an image on screen representing a program, file, folder or particular function.
Menu – a list of possible options.

Common misconceptions

● The GUI system was not invented by Microsoft. It was actually invented by Xerox Corporation's research division, PARC during the 1970s.
● Microsoft Windows works with MS-DOS and is not, as many people believe, a complete replacement.

Questions

Should I upgrade to Windows 2000?
A computer is a tool like any other and until there comes a time when it is not able to do its job, it should be left. Upgrades are only really necessary if software incompatibilities become a problem. For example, those school's machines running Windows 3.1 will find many new software packages incompatible and so an upgrade is desirable. However, Windows 95 and Windows 98 machines are for the moment more than sufficient. New purchases should, however, always be the most recent versions.

If I delete a program shortcut, will I be deleting the program?
Shortcuts can be made to programs, folders and individual files. Deleting these is very easy and will not delete the actual program, folder or file. Simply place your mouse over the shortcut icon, click the right button and click on *Delete*.

Golden rules

● Only ever rename files and folders you have created yourself, otherwise programs may not function correctly.
● Always apply some degree of desktop security for the classroom computer. Changes are very easily made by inquiring minds. Access to Windows Explorer should be denied to all pupils.

● Although deleted files are put in the Recycle Bin where they may be rescued at a later date, it is important to remember that the recycle bin will start to empty itself once it gets to a certain capacity (usually 10 per cent of your hard disk). Files are deleted on a first in, first out basis.

● If you're trying to find a character that doesn't appear on your keyboard, simply use the Character Map which can be found in the *Accessories* menu.

● When transferring files between home and work, use the My Briefcase facility, which automatically updates your files. For example, if you start work on a document at school and then decide to carry on at home, using the briefcase facility will mean that your school file will be updated with the additional data when you return. Here's how it could work:

4pm	*Finish working on policy document. Decide to take it home for some additional work.*
	Open Windows Explorer and drag the file to the My Briefcase *icon.*
	Insert your floppy disk.
	Right-click on the My Briefcase *icon.*
	Select Send To *(and select the appropriate drive, usually A: for the floppy drive).*
7pm	*At home. Start work on policy document.*
	Insert floppy disk.
	Open Windows Explorer.
	Click A: drive icon.
	Double-click on the My Briefcase *icon.*
	Open your file by double-clicking on it.
	Remember to save any changes you make.
8am	*Back at school. Decide to finish off policy document.*
	Insert floppy disk.
	Open Windows Explorer.
	Double-click on My Briefcase *icon.*
	Select Update All.
	Check file details.
	Click on Update *button.*

Your file should now be updated ready for you to continue.

● If you're finding double-clicking difficult it may be because the speed setting is too high. The Accessibility Options in the Control Panel let you change this.

● If you find yourself stuck, try Windows' help facility which can be found in the *Start* menu. Search the index for your problem.

● If you use a particular program frequently, create a shortcut to it from your desktop. This will mean that you do not have to go through the different menus to locate your program as an icon will be placed directly onto your desktop. To do this, open Windows Explorer and reduce the size of the window so that you can still see your desktop. Find your program and, while placing the pointer over it, click the right mouse button. From the menu select *Create shortcut*. A new icon should be created; select this and drag it to the desktop. Every time you double-click this new icon, it will take you directly to your chosen program.

Multimedia software

Subject facts

What is multimedia software?

Multimedia software combines text, images, sound, animation and video all on screen. Whilst a particular multimedia title does not have to include all the above elements, it will have a selected combination. A CD-ROM on animals, for example, could contain not only colour photos and text (as a printed book can) but film of animals in real life surroundings and recordings of the sounds they make. Finding the right information is easy too: just click on the list of animals or type in a name – far simpler for children who struggle to use an index or contents list. Information can also be printed out or copied into a word-processing program so it is part of a larger piece of work.

Making it possible

Multimedia was only made possible with the invention of the CD-ROM and its ability to store large amounts of data. When it was first invented, it was able to store more than twice the amount of data that a standard desktop computer could handle. With this greater capacity, large video and sound files were able to be stored on a single CD-ROM. The age of multimedia and interactive software had begun.

The multimedia PC

To take advantage of all the new features of multimedia software, compatible hardware is required. Firstly, a CD-ROM drive is essential, together with speakers and the necessary components inside your PC, namely a capable sound card and graphics card. The latter two will ensure that the graphics and sound files are reproduced to an acceptable standard. Upgrade kits are available for older machines while newer ones will come with the necessary equipment as standard.

Interactivity

Multimedia software can also be highly interactive. Navigation in a non-linear fashion is made possible using hypertext and hotspots. Pupils soon become adept at locating these and hopping from one link to another.

Advantages of interactivity

● It empowers the user, who can make choices and follow their own learning path.
● It allows users to learn at their own pace.
● Different types of media mean that the user can choose one that appeals to him or her.

Multimedia software is playing a vital role in the educational environment. Put together with the ever-increasing presence of the Internet, with its endless multimedia on tap, getting to grips with the technologies and harnessing its learning potential is going to prove more and more crucial.

Why you need to know these facts

Plug and play – new technology that makes the installation of new equipment much simpler.
Seek time – the amount of time taken by a laser beam to locate data on a CD-ROM.
Data transfer times – the time taken to transfer data from the CD-ROM to the computer.
Acronyms
K/s – Kilobytes per second.

Vocabulary

● Windows 98 comes with over 1000 drivers that will recognize over 1000 peripheral devices.
● The trend towards an all-in-one system where a PC is combined with a television is set to continue and likely to take over the home market in the near future.
● One screen-sized photographic image requires the same amount of storage as the book you are reading now.
● A single CD-ROM has enough storage capacity to hold the text of the *Encyclopaedia Britannica* twice over!
● Whilst the performance rates of CD-ROMs have improved since the 1980s, their storage capacity has

Amazing facts

remained constant at 650Mb. However, research is under way to produce a double-sided disc that will be able to store up to 9000Mb of data!

What's the difference between a double-speed CD-ROM drive and a quad-speed drive?

A double-speed CD-ROM has a data transfer rate of 300K/s whereas a quad-speed drive spins twice as fast and has a transfer rate of 600K/s – twice as fast. It is now possible to get forty- and even fifty-speed CD-ROM drives, with transfer rates in excess of 6000K/s.

I've installed a CD-ROM encyclopaedia onto my computer; will I still need the CD-ROM?

Yes, the installation procedure will not have put all the data onto your hard drive and so you will need to put the CD-ROM into the drive so that the software can access relevant data when it needs to. Just as well really, as you probably wouldn't have much space for anything else.

Always handle CD-ROMs carefully, holding them around the edges. A deep scratch can be fatal.

● Ask pupils to wear headphones when exploring distracting multimedia titles. Check that the sound level is appropriate for each pupil, particularly those known to have hearing difficulties.

● You can change the screen settings on most CD-ROMs so that text is easier to read. Changing the colour of text and backgrounds can make it easier for young readers and those with impaired vision.

TEEM (Teachers Evaluating Educational Multimedia) www.teem.org.uk – If you're not sure about which multimedia title to buy for school, this site can help. Each title is trialled by volunteer teachers and then given an objective assessment.

Chapter 3

Applications

To integrate ICT within the curriculum, teachers need to have a good understanding of major applications software. At Key Stage 1, integration is only required with the core subjects; at Key Stage 2, ICT will need to be integrated with all curriculum subjects except for physical education.

It is only when teachers become sufficiently familiar with the necessary applications that any creative and educationally worthwhile integration will develop. It is the aim of this chapter to get teachers well on their way to achieving this by looking more closely at word processing software, spreadsheets, databases, multimedia, drawing and other useful software packages.

Word processing

Subject facts

The word processor has to be one of the most widely experienced types of application in computing. It has relegated typewriters to the status of antiquated artefact, and this has happened in a surprisingly short amount of time – some of the very youngest children may never have seen a typewriter at all! Without a doubt, word processing has opened up the possibilities and benefits of printed text to virtually anyone, and whilst typing skills are a distinct advantage, they are not essential.

Advantages of printed text

Whilst no one will disagree that content is more important than presentation, there is little doubt that presentation can have a real impact on both the reader and writer. Instilling a sense of pride in their work is of paramount importance when trying to motivate pupils.

Many pupils struggle with handwriting – deciding what they want to say, working out how to spell it, and producing neatly formed letters all at the same time can be a tall order. Dyslexic children and those with special needs face even greater problems. Using a word processor places them on a more even footing with others; whilst keyboard skills also need mastering, the outcome of a keystroke is far less subjective than that of handwritten text. The process of re-drafting is also far less of a chore, and when pupils are taught and encouraged to utilize some of the more advanced editing tools, it can in fact be fun. Even the most reluctant writer can be motivated to extend their writing, and improve on their earlier efforts.

A time and place

With the increase in ICT hardware available in classrooms, pupils are word-processing more and more of their work. The use of a word processor needs to be justified, however, just as any other activity in the classroom. Producing every piece of work on a word processor would not only prove practically impossible, but would also be inappropriate. Writing for different purposes and audiences will help determine the method used.

Drafting longer poems and narrative texts, for example, is an appropriate task for word processing once the pupil has acquired basic keyboarding skills and is able to type with some fluency and speed. As the first draft will be saved, there is no need to rewrite chunks of text when editing. Pupils will also benefit from using tools such as the spellchecker and thesaurus.

On the other hand, a brainstorming activity would not be an appropriate use of a word processor. Pupils would find it difficult to recreate the layout of a brainstorm on screen. This in turn would confuse and distract from the thought processes that a brainstorm is hoping to promote.

Formatting

One of the distinct advantages of computer-created documents is the ease with which they can be altered. Formatting involves selecting the font and size of text, emboldening, italicizing or underlining it, and aligning it on the page. Most word processors make formatting as easy as clicking a button, though as with most other computer programs, they tend to have more than one way of achieving the same effect. Remember that you always need to highlight the text you wish to format *before* you enter the changes to be made.

Keyboard shortcuts for formatting text using Microsoft Word

Task	Quick Code Using Microsoft Word
Changes lower case to upper case and vice versa (very useful when you've forgotten to turn CAPS LOCK off!)	SHIFT+F3
Calls up formatting dialogue box	CTRL+D
Emboldens selected text	CTRL+B
Underlines selected text	CTRL+U
Italicises text	CTRL+I
Applies small capitals to selected text	CTRL+SHIFT+K
Double underline text	CTRL+SHIFT+D
Increases size of selected text by 2 points each time	CTRL+SHIFT+>
Decreases size of selected text by 2 points each time	CTRL+SHIFT+<
Copies the formatting of the selected text	CTRL+SHIFT+C
Applies copied formatting to selected text	CTRL+SHIFT+V
Undoes last action	CTRL+Z
Re-does last action	CTRL+Y
Applies subscript	CTRL+=
Applies superscript	CTRL+SHIFT+=
Applies all caps	CTRL+SHIFT+A

Tabs and spaces

It's worth mastering the *Tabs* and *Indents* features if you want to produce lists or columns of text. In Microsoft Word, experiment with the ruler at the top of the page and you can indent text and create decimal tabs too.

Editing text

Apart from formatting text, editing facilities can turn even the non-typist in to a proficient word processor. Text can be deleted, inserted, copied and moved around with relative ease. Windows users will also find that uniformity between programs will help when learning these essential skills, as once learned for one Windows program, they can be applied to others too.

Deleting text

There are several ways to delete text. If the cursor is directly in front (to the right) of the word you wish to delete, the best option is to use the BACKSPACE key. Pressing this will move the cursor backwards deleting anything that comes in its way. To delete whole sentences or paragraphs, use the DELETE key. First highlight the text you wish to delete with the mouse and then press the DELETE or BACKSPACE keys. Remember, if using the DELETE key to delete single letters or words without highlighting, place the cursor to the left of the text.

Moving text

There are two main methods by which text can be moved in a document: copy and paste and cut and paste. When a word or paragraph is copied, a copy of the selected text is sent to the clipboard with the original remaining in place. The copy that has been placed on the clipboard may then be pasted anywhere in the document by placing the cursor in the desired position and then selecting *Paste* from the *Edit* menu (see below for a quicker way of doing this). When a word is cut, a copy is once again sent to the clipboard but this time the original is removed from the text. To paste the contents of the clipboard to another position, place the cursor in the desired spot and select *Paste* from the *Edit* menu again.

Keyboard shortcuts for Microsoft Word

Task	Shortcut
Cuts text from document	CTRL+X
Copies text to clipboard	CTRL+C
Pastes items from the clipboard	CTRL+V
Activates spellchecker	F7
Activates thesaurus	SHIFT+F7

You can also move text from one document to another. Having copied or cut the text, simply open another document and paste the text into it as before.

Templates

A template is quite simply the framework of a document that is intended to be used repeatedly. A template will include text and formatting that needs to remain constant (such as a letterhead) and provide the user with a quick and easy method of customizing the template for different circumstances. Imagine, for example, having to write 45 thank you letters all in one go. Each letter would share common elements: your name and address at the top of the letter, the date and perhaps even an introductory paragraph. Without a template you would have to type these in for each letter in turn.

If, however, a template was created with these common elements included, all that would be required would be the additional text for the letter, which could be personalized for each recipient. Importantly, once you have created your template, anything you add to it will not permanently change it, as long as you save the new customized document as a normal word processor file. So, once you have thanked auntie Kay, you simply save the file as a normal document with a new filename and start a new letter with your original template which will have the bare bones structure ready to thank someone else. Thus, templates not only cut down on the time needed to create customized documents, but also reduce the risk of errors as, once checked and saved, the common elements will remain unchangeable.

---

22 Oak St
Denton
7FG 2GG

Dear
Thanks for your very generous gift.

Love
Avy

Saved as template called 'Thank you letter'

---

22 Oak St
Denton
7FG 2GG

Dear Remy,
Thanks for your very generous gift.
I was hoping to receive a new pair of gloves as my old ones have become a bit tatty. I was really pleased that you got me some in my favourite colour. I will wear them next time I'm out in the cold.

Love
Avy

Resaved as a normal document called remy.doc

Saving a document as a template

Once you have created a document that you wish to save as a template, you must make sure it is saved as a template in the *Save As* dialogue box from the *File* menu. When you name the file in the dialogue box, there will be a list of options marked *Save File as Type;* to save a template, choose *Document Template* from this list.

The spellchecker

For many people, the spellchecker has been a real life-saver. Most word processors now offer this utility as standard, often whilst you are actually typing. However, the spellchecker is not infallible, and pupils need to be taught the necessary skills in order to use it effectively. The principle behind a spellchecker is actually quite simple and this goes some way to explaining its shortcomings.

A spellchecker has a database of words which will be used to check against possible errors. If a word does not appear in the spellchecker's database it will be flagged up as a possible error, and the corrections suggested will be the nearest match to the original word typed. A spellchecker is unable to take in to account context, and this inability to act intelligently is what makes spellcheckers fall short of many people's expectations. To a spellchecker, for example, the words *see* and *sea* are both legitimate, but the context will determine which is correct.

Advantages of a spellchecker	Example
Picks up common spelling errors	It wass a colde day.
Picks up on missed spaces Helps pupils edit their own work	She couldn't waitfor her birthda ysurprise.
Disadvantages of a spellchecker	**Example**
Dependent upon a database of words that often does not include names and colloquialisms	Whoops! said Margy when she dropped her hat.
Unable to spot correctly spelled mis-used words	It was not fare that too children were left out inn the cold.

Customizing your spellchecker

To stop the annoyance of regularly used, correctly spelled words being picked up by your spellchecker, add them to the spellchecker's database. In Microsoft Word this is done by selecting the *Add* button in the spellchecker. (You may also need to check that it is set to UK English rather than US, to prevent *color* being confused with *colour*. Check this by looking at *Preferences* under the *Tools* menu.)

The thesaurus

The electronic thesaurus available on many word processors today works very much like its paper counterpart. It offers a list of synonyms which may or may not be used to replace the original word. It must be stressed, however, that just like the spellchecker, the thesaurus is not a magic wand and requires an intelligent response by the user. Also, before the list of synonyms may be considered, the user needs to check the grammatical context of the word. For example, the word *trip* may be used as a verb, as in *The boy is likely to trip over his laces*, or it may be used as a noun, as in *She had a wonderful school trip*. Unless the correct context is used, the list of suggested synonyms may be very confusing.

What is a word bank?

A word bank is a collection of words that can be provided for pupils to use when word processing. Younger children who are slow at typing in text will simply need to select words from the word bank using their mouse and use the copy and paste function to add the word to their writing. This added support will encourage younger pupils and speed up what may have been a very lengthy process. Older pupils and those with physical impairments will also benefit from word banks which will direct their attention to the use of specific vocabulary.

Integrating ICT

In these examples, the links with language are obvious and the ICT connection is transparent. Many teachers, however, overlook the opportunities of a double-edged learning objective. Word-processing skills should not be conceptualized or taught out of context. A lesson on adjectives could be incorporated with a look at a word processor's thesaurus. A lesson on letter-writing would work well with a look at formatting text. A study of different fonts could be given artistic, creative and historical perspectives.

Report writing in science is another area where pupils could design their own templates for use throughout the year. These need not always be filled in at the computer; they could be photocopied and handwritten.

Why you need to know these facts

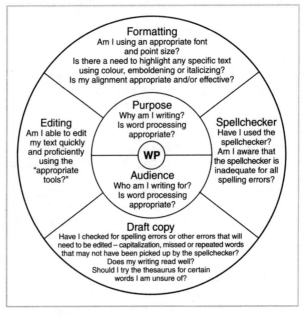

Word-processing skills should be developed with a mind to good practice, incorporating the development of keyboard skills, efficient use of editing, appropriate use of formatting, and with an awareness of purpose and audience at all times.

Golden rules

● Word processors work on proportional spacing (where characters only take us as much space as they need: 'i' takes up less space than 'm', for example), so if you simply add spaces to try and line up words, you're likely to get a ragged edge. Use the TAB key instead.
● Always use the SHIFT key for single capital letters as opposed to the CAPS LOCK key. It is good practice!
● Many word processors have different language settings, so make sure that you have selected UK English as opposed to American English or any other that may be on offer to avoid confusion between 'color' and 'colour'. This may affect your spellchecker, and may mean that your keyboard types some of the wrong characters!

- If you only wish to spellcheck one particular word, simply highlight it and then activate the spellchecker.
- Where possible, create themed word banks for topic work in advance.
- Unless encroaching on your specific learning objectives, use templates when you want pupils to follow specific standard layouts – for letter writing, science reports and so on. Not only will this save time, it will also help pupils to focus on their writing.
- Print out examples of the fonts available on the classroom computer so that pupils can consult these before going on to the computer. While they may still wish to try out fonts, they can eliminate their least favourite choices in advance.
- Use Windows' Character Map to copy and paste symbols which are not available on your keyboard into your document. The 'Wingdings' font contains lots of useful graphical images including religious symbols and clock faces. To insert characters into a document, select any special characters you wish by highlighting them in Character Map and then clicking on *Select*. Once you have made your selection, click on *Copy*. Your selections are now saved to the clipboard ready to be pasted wherever you wish them to be.
- If you want to highlight all the text in your document but find the manual method tricky, simply go to the *Edit* menu and click on *Select All*.
- If you want to count the number of words in a document, pull down the *Tools* menu and select *Word count*.

Amazing facts

- Did you know that Microsoft Word has no less than nine English dialects included in its options? These include dialects from Britain, Canada, the USA, New Zealand, Australia, the Caribbean, Jamaica, Ireland and South Africa.
- When Bill Gates demonstrated the first ever version of Microsoft Word it contained well over 100 bugs!
- Microsoft Word is able to increase the font size to 1638 points – that would produce a letter over 22 inches high!

Questions

What is the difference between serif and sans serif fonts?
A serif font is one whose letters have little lines or curves projecting from the ascenders and descenders, such as the font you are reading now. A sans serif font is one which has no lines or curves projecting from the ascenders and descenders, such as the one at the top of this page. The

latter uses the French word *sans* meaning 'without'. Young
readers are thought to find serif fonts easier to read, but you
can also buy child-friendly fonts such as 'Sassoon', which
emulate rounded handwriting.

Can I start writing text on a new page even if I haven't finished the previous one?

Yes, in Microsoft Word simply place the cursor at the end of
the last line of text and press CTRL+ENTER, or go to the *Insert*
menu and select *Break*.

I have Microsoft Word version 6 at home. Can I open my files at school using Word 97 and vice versa?

Compatibility within different versions of the same program
can be problematic. The main thing to remember is that
programs are nearly always downwardly compatible: this
means that a newer version can handle files produced on
older versions but not the other way around. So, whilst you
will have no problem accessing your home files at school,
files created at school on the newer version will need to be
saved as a version 6 document. This is easily done in the
Save As dialogue box: simply select the *Word for Windows 6*
format in the *Save File as Type* option box.

What's a hanging indent?

If you want to align your text away from the left-hand
margin (where you have a numbered list or bullets, for
example), use a hanging indent. In Microsoft Word, use the
Tabs dialogue box in the *Format* menu.

Can I scan text into my word-processing program?

It is possible to scan text into a word processor if your
scanner has Optical Character Recognition (OCR) software.
This is not perfect but is improving all the time. See the
section on peripheral input devices (page 19).

All change!

Prepare short pieces of text that require editing. Save the
original as a template so that each pupil can carry out the
editing, and ask them to save their work with an
appropriate file name.

All jumbled up

To give young pupils practice in cutting and pasting, enter
the lines of a familiar rhyme into the word processor in the

wrong order and ask pupils to put them right. Alternatively, they could try sequencing by putting common tasks through the day in the correct order (waking up, getting dressed, going to school, having lunch and so on).

Happy birthday to who?

As part of an exercise on formatting, give groups of two or three children a piece of unformatted text that needs to be changed into a birthday invitation. Give groups additional information relating to the audience and time to prepare before they actually start work on the computer. Instruct pupils that no additional text is permitted. A short discussion at the beginning on marking changes to the text may be helpful, though it is not necessary for the class to come up with a standard form. Hopefully, groups will come up with different styles depending on their audience and these can be displayed. To finish off, ask groups to guess each other's audience.

Read all about it!

In small groups, give pupils different types of newspaper. Prepare a questionnaire that focuses on the layout, different fonts used, and other formatting techniques that have been implemented. Some example questions would be:

How many different fonts have been used?
Are there any fonts that are difficult to read?
What can you say about headline text?
How many columns has your newspaper got?
Is all the text the same size?
Apart from the size of text, what other techniques have been used to get the reader's attention?
Has colour been used? How?
Have graphic elements (such as boxes, shapes and lines) been used?
What type of audience do you think is being targetted?

Ask each group to study their newspaper and fill in their questionnaires. As a plenary, groups report back on their findings.

Using a thesaurus

Prepare a list of sentences using simple language that have the potential to be improved, for example *The girl walked along the path.* Colour the word *walked* so that it stands out. Ask pupils to use the thesaurus to change the word *walked* to a different one. Compare work done by different groups.

Resources

Software

Clicker 3 – an excellent word processor for younger users, and for those who have difficulty with the keyboard. Pupils can simply point and click on any word, letter, picture or sound to have it incorporated into their page. The word banks can be created with ease and teachers can decide how much or little assistance is given. Available from Crick Software (tel: 01604 671691, www.cricksoft.com).

Write Away – an educational word processor that can be used at different levels. Includes many additional tools including a spellchecker, on-screen word banks which can be customized and a fun word game to reinforce correct spelling. Available from suppliers of educational software.

Write on – another word processor specifically aimed at the educational market, which has four different user levels and its spellchecker can speak the suggested words in a choice of 20 different voices. Available from SPA software (tel: 01684 833700, www.spasoft.com).

StartWrite – word-process your own handwriting sheets. A word processor that will print letters in dots or dashes ready for pupils to write over. Lots of additional features to make customizing handwriting sheets easy. Available from Sherston Software (tel: 01666 843200, www.sherston.com).

Books

Primarily IT: Using IT to support English, maths and science at KS2 – this publication includes primary case studies and examples of pupils' work, together with highlighting appropriate curriculum links and the specific contribution of ICT. Produced by Becta (tel: 024 7641 6994, www.becta.org.uk).

Websites

Newman College Curriculum Links – www.newman.ac.uk/links.html

Kidpub – www.kidpub.org – a wonderful site that is devoted to publishing children's stories. What better way to motivate your pupils?

Free fonts – www.1001freefonts.com – a great collection of free fonts for you to download. If you are a Windows user, use the Control Panel to install the new fonts.

What is a spreadsheet?

An electronic spreadsheet is based on its paper predecessor. It is made up of rows and columns that form the basis of data organization. Individual cells are given unique cell references which are of paramount importance when utilizing formulae.

Types of entry

Cells may have three types of data input: labels, values and formulae. Labels consist of text; values are numbers and formulae make calculations. The advantages of formulae in electronic spreadsheets have not only made them an indispensable tool in the commercial world but also a valid educational tool in schools.

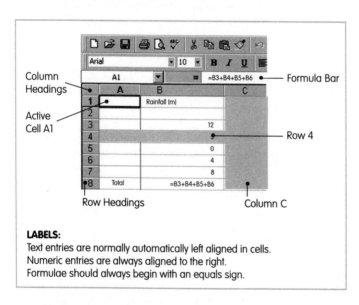

LABELS:
Text entries are normally automatically left aligned in cells.
Numeric entries are always aligned to the right.
Formulae should always begin with an equals sign.

Moving around and selecting cells

It is normally possible to choose between the mouse and the keyboard to navigate around and select cells. Pupils who have difficulty with the mouse may find the keyboard a better option.

Formatting numeric entries

Considerable care must be taken when entering numerical data. Numeric entries contain the values which formulae use and, if inaccurate, problems will occur later. Unless specifically formatted, all numeric entries will be treated as straightforward values. However, times, dates, telephone numbers and monetary values are clearly not. Some numeric entries will require specific formatting. Important ones to remember would be date and time entries and money; telephone numbers, though not strictly a number, will also need special treatment. Formatting a number just means that it is recognized for what it is. For example, 12.50 formatted as a time will be treated as ten to one, rather than twelve and a half.

Writing simple formulae

Formulae enable pupils to make automatic calculations instantaneously, and as formulae work with cell references and not numbers they are able to recalculate themselves when the values in the cells change.

The most common mathematical operators used in spreadsheet formulae are:

^	*to the power of*	*example*	*=2^3*
+	*add*	*example*	*=3+4*
-	*minus*	*example*	*=4-3*
/	*divided by*	*example*	*=4/2*
*	*multiplied by*	*example*	*=3*3*

Note that, in order to keep entries simple, some of the operation symbols used are different to those used in conventional mathematics, and all formulae begin with an equals sign.

However, as with convention, values in brackets are always worked out first, and care should be taken to establish any operator precedence system your particular spreadsheet program may adhere to. Microsoft Excel, for instance, multiplies and divides before it adds and subtracts. So, if you wanted a formula to add a set of numbers and then divide you would need to place the numbers you wanted to add first in brackets. For example:

$$=(C4+D4+E4+F4+G4+H4)/2$$

An even quicker way to key in this formula would be to use a colon to indicate a range, for example:

$$=(C4:H4)/2$$

And of course don't forget you can use the mouse to select cells, which is usually even quicker and more accurate. By clicking in the desired cell, its cell reference is automatically placed in the formula bar without additional typing.

Relative and absolute cell references

We have already mentioned that formulae are created using cell references. However, a cell reference in a formula can either be relative or absolute. The concept behind relative and absolute cell references can be a little confusing at first, but with a little practice and lots of examples for pupils, their existence will be acknowledged as being logical, necessary and practical.

Study the following spreadsheet:

	A	B	C
1	Rate of pay	£3.50	Daily pay
2	Day	Hrs worked	
3	Mon	8	=B3*B1
4	Tue	7	
5	Wed	9	
6	Thu	6	
7	Fri	6	

The dollar sign around the second cell reference indicates that it is an absolute cell reference.

The formula in cell C3 includes both a relative cell reference (B3) and an absolute cell reference (B1). The absolute cell reference means that only the number in cell B1 may be used as this value. This is an absolute value and will never change regardless of where the formula is entered or later moved to. However, B3 is a relative cell reference. In other words, depending on where the formula is pasted it may not always be the value in B3 that is used in the formula. The original relative cell reference indicates that it will always be the value of the cell that is one cell to the left of where the formula is pasted. Therefore if the formula was pasted down to C4, the formula would automatically use the value in B4, as this is now the cell immediately to the left of the formula. Practice will overcome the confusion!

Formatting your spreadsheet

Once a spreadsheet has been used to generate some useful
information, it should be used to present this in a clear and
easy to understand format. Pupils need to be shown how to
format the data in cells appropriately. If you are using a
Windows-based program, formatting skills will be easily
transferable from previous work.

	A	B	C	D	E
1		Breakfast Survey			
2		Milk	Cereal	Tea	Toast
3	Mon	21	66	1	98
4	Tue	23	78	5	112
5	Wed	11	75	3	67
6	Thu	32	56	0	43
7	Fri	12	45	4	87
8	TOTAL	99	320	13	407

Title enlarged and emboldened
Totals boxes shaded to highlight their importance.
Labels emboldened and centred. Make sure all labels
are same size and font.
Use of capitalization to draw attention to important
information

Formatting Dos and Don'ts

ALWAYS	NEVER
Preserve a degree of consistency with labels and headings.	Use too many different fonts in one spreadsheet.
Choose appropriate fonts; fancy fonts are better suited to more creative projects.	Overdo the colours! Remember your aim is to make the information clear and aesthetically pleasing at the same time.
Remember to emphasize key pieces of information by simple techniques such as highlighting, emboldening or increasing font size.	Overpower the data.

Too much fancy formatting can overpower the actual data.
Formatting needs to assist in highlighting and clarifying key
data, not obscuring it.

Functions

Once pupils are confident with writing simple formulae they can be introduced to some basic functions that are normally included in all good spreadsheet programs.

A function is an automated shortcut to writing a formula. Rather than devising a formula from scratch, you simply select the function that will carry out the calculation you need. Functions save time and minimize errors.

Parts of a function

A function is normally made up of three parts. In this example:

$$=sum(A1:A8)$$

the parts are the function name, a set of parentheses and arguments, or data.

It is important that the function name is spelt correctly and is preceded by an equals sign. A set of parentheses is used to enclose the function's arguments. The arguments provide the vital data required for the function; without these no calculation could be performed. A function without arguments is a little like a recipe without the ingredients.

Although a program such as Microsoft Excel has over 300 different kinds of function, work in the primary classroom need only utilize a fraction of these.

Name of Function	What it does	Working example
SUM	Arithmetic addition	Adding numbers sold
PRODUCT	Multiplication of two numbers	Working out revenue raised: number of sales × price of item
AVERAGE	Arithmetic mean of a set of numbers	Average shoe size in class
MODE	Most frequently occurring value in a data series	Sales of favourite sweets in tuck shop.
MEDIAN	The middle value in a data series	Prices of mid-range items in tuck shop's range of items sold
MIN	Identifies the smallest value in a given list of arguments	Cheapest item in the school tuck shop
MAX	Identifies the greatest value in a given list of arguments	Tallest child in the school

Graphs and charts

One of the great advantages of a spreadsheet program is the ease with which the user can create graphs and charts which would otherwise have been difficult, or even impossible, to produce.

Graphs and charts assist in the assimilation of data – particularly when you are faced with an enormous amount of numerical data. When using an appropriate graph or chart, patterns and relationships are far easier to spot than they would have been otherwise.

Choosing an appropriate graph or chart

Whilst some of the more sophisticated spreadsheet programs offer many different types of graphs and charts there are in essence only four basic types: bar chart, pie chart, line graph and scatter graph. All others are variations on these. However, choosing the right type of chart or graph is a mathematical skill that pupils need to be taught and is not purely a case of personal preference. Showing pupils the pros and cons of different charts and graphs enables them to choose appropriate ones for different purposes independently. In primary schools the most important types are the bar chart, pie chart, line graph and scatter graph.

Bar chart

A bar chart is excellent for showing direct comparisons between different sets of data. A bar chart would be the best option to show, for example, the results of a class survey on favourite colours:

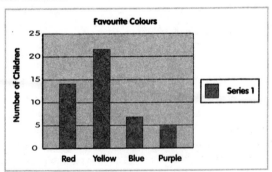

Pie chart

In simple terms a pie chart shows how something has been shared out. Each segment represents a fraction of the total. For example, a pie chart could show the percentage of a pupil's pocket money being spent on sweets, toys and savings:

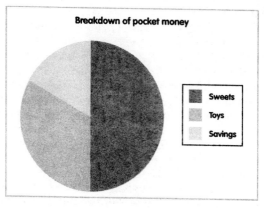

Line graph

Line graphs are often used to show changes over time. Line graphs are particularly useful in science investigations where, for example, temperature readings are measured over a period of time:

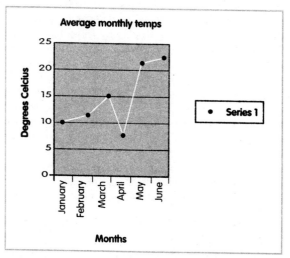

Scatter graphs

One of the least-used types of graph which can in fact produce the most telling visual representations of data is the scatter graph. Scatter graphs are excellent at showing the relationship of two different sets of data, and simply consist of a set of points. At least two different quantities are plotted against one another to investigate whether a relationship between the two exists. Scatter graphs are good for investigating simple hypotheses such as *The taller a person is, the bigger their shoe size.*

Integrating ICT

The links with mathematics are obvious – spreadsheets are a great way to introduce simple equation and formula problems. Number patterns can be explored in a more dynamic way and, while it is vital that we teach pupils to be independently numerate, there are times when a computer can eliminate the drudgery of mental calculation so that other, possibly more explorative, mathematics can be pursued.

Spreadsheets can also be used in many other areas. In geography, you can input data relating to weather and climate which will produce very impressive charts and graphs. In history, make comparative studies of birth and death rates during different periods in history, average wages, school leaving ages – the list is endless.

Spreadsheets in science can be invaluable tools to show the results of investigations graphically. Consider using a spreadsheet to plot results of a science investigation into the thermal properties of differing materials. Temperature readings are recorded using a spreadsheet and different graphs can be produced. The results of different variables can also be plotted on one chart and a graphical representation is always easier to understand than raw numbers. Revitalize the old shadow clock investigation by using a spreadsheet to show the results graphically.

| Why you need to know these facts | Spreadsheets are an excellent way for teachers to introduce and develop pupils' skills of computer-aided modelling. By Key Stage 2 the National Curriculum specifically mentions the exploration of the 'What if…?' scenario and spreadsheets are an excellent and accessible tool for this. |

Amazing facts

● The commercial success of the Apple Macintosh since 1984 has often been attributed to the popularity of Microsoft Excel. Many people bought a Macintosh purely because of Excel and the facilities it offered. Together with Aldus Pagemaker, which made the Macintosh an almost independent print studio, it could be said that Excel saved the Macintosh from the fate of obscurity that had befallen its predecessor, the Lisa.

● A single Microsoft Excel spreadsheet can have up to 256 vertical columns and 16 384 rows: that's 4194 304 cells in total!

● Always format telephone numbers correctly. This is particularly important if the telephone number begins with a zero. Without formatting, the number will be seen as a standard numerical entry and the first zero will disappear, as it will be regarded as superfluous.

● Make sure the organization of your spreadsheet clearly distinguishes between a numeric entry and a text entry. Cells included in a formula must be numeric entries. The following is an example of bad organization and these cells could not be used in a formula as they are not purely numeric entries.

| Mon | 7 Biscuits sold |
| Tue | 9 Biscuits sold |

A better way to organize your spreadsheet would be to use clearly numeric entries that can be included in a formula, as below:

Day	No. of biscuits sold
Mon	7
Tue	9

● Whenever you want to have a series of numbers – be it dates, days of the week or consecutive numbers – check whether you can use *auto fill,* which will save a lot of tedious typing and reduce typing errors. It's well worth spending a few minutes to investigate.

● Save time and increase your accuracy by copying formulae. For example, if a 15% discount needs to be calculated on a set of prices, the formula need only be typed once and then copied down the column.

● To remember the order in which calculations are performed in many spreadsheets, remember BODMAS:

B = brackets; O = ordinals; D = division;
M = multiplication; A = addition; S = subtraction.

● Make a large sign around the ICT area in your classroom listing the rules concerning formulae, such as to always start a formula with an = sign, never to include empty cells in a formula, to remember to use curved brackets not squared, list the order of operator precedence your spreadsheet software may adhere to and so on.

Applications

● Formulae breathe life into spreadsheets and children are excited by this seemingly magical aspect. The ability of the computer to calculate such large numbers so quickly and recalculate when changes are made creates a real sense of doing something quite difficult that perhaps they wouldn't have been able to do unaided. And isn't this what computers are for?

● As with most computer-related activities, there is always more than one way of doing something, and spreadsheet formulae are no different. However, introduce techniques slowly and let the pupils set the pace. Using the keyboard method to enter data into a formula may be the best option for an inexperienced mouse user. There will come a time when your pupils will feel comfortable enough to enquire about a quicker or better way and this would be the best time to introduce alternatives.

● A common mistake when introducing spreadsheet formulae is to introduce too many new learning objectives. If introducing formulae for the first time, concentrate on only that learning objective. Keep the context simple, use simple numbers and do not simultaneously introduce new mathematical concepts that will confuse pupils unnecessarily. There is, of course, nothing wrong with using spreadsheets to explore new mathematical concepts but this will only prove successful after the fundamentals of spreadsheets are mastered.

● Using the PRINT SCREEN option, print out blank or prepared spreadsheet forms that can be used for desk-based activities. Remember, a lot of ICT can be done away from the computer. If you wish to leave a blank cell for pupils to write in formulae, remember to increase the width of the cell to provide enough space.

● Ask pupils to devise a formula that will create certain number patterns. Try arithmetic progressions, such as 2 4 6 8 10 12 14 16, and geometric progressions like 2 4 8 16 32 64. As with most problem-solving activities, there are a number of different solutions. Ask pupils to use relative cell references to start off with and then absolute cell references. Extend the more able pupils and ask for all possible solutions and then discuss the efficiency of each.

● Prepare in advance simple financial scenarios, leaving out the required formulae. Try, say, the weekly accounts of the school tuck shop, or monthly accounts for 'Mr Pump's Sports Shop'. The formulae can be filled in at the desk and tested at the computer.

● Challenge pupils to come up with formulae that generate

specific number patterns associated with the work of famous mathematicians, such as Fibonacci and Pascal. Once inspired, let pupils come up with formulae that generate their own number patterns, and turn the exercise into a quiz – let pupils try to work out the correct formula for each number pattern. This type of explorative mathematics will encourage the less able and challenge the more able.

What is a formula?

This abstract concept is tricky to explain to pupils. Try explaining a formula as a way of writing a special rule that has to be followed exactly to get the right result – rather like a recipe which sets down all the instructions for a cook.

Why do formulae always have to begin with an = sign?

The = sign simply lets the computer know that the entry is a formula and therefore it should be treated as such. It could have been any symbol but thankfully a norm has been established, and with all industry-standard spreadsheet programs the = sign is used.

Can you name groups of related data for a formula?

Obviously it depends on your particular software, but normally the answer is yes. You can group a set of cells and give them a name which can then be used in a formula.

Shoe size
4
6
5
5

Once assigned as the name for these cells, this alone need appear in a formula, making things quicker and easier.

What's the difference between an absolute cell reference and a relative cell reference?

This really is a tricky concept to grasp and will need lots of practical work to reinforce. Basically, the value assigned by an absolute cell reference *never* changes. It is constant throughout, regardless of where the formula is placed. However, the value assigned by a relative cell reference is dependent upon the position relative to the original formula – maybe 1 cell to the left; even 1 cell to the left and 2 up!

When is a number not a number?

One of the most important lessons to be learned when working with computers is the need to be very precise and absolutely logical. Computers are as yet not very good at assimilating information, although programmers are constantly working at making them more and more intuitive. When a spreadsheet works with a number it needs to be a number in the strictest sense. Try entering a telephone number that starts with a zero, and it will always be knocked off as the computer will see it as superfluous. Date and time entries are also similar examples. These sorts of special numerical entries therefore need to be formatted so that they are recognized for what they are and treated in the appropriate manner.

Resources

Software

RM Number Magic – tailor-made spreadsheet program for primary schools. Includes many features that make it an excellent choice for younger pupils. Available from RM (tel: 01235 826000, www.rm.com).
Number Box – Educational spreadsheet for Windows. Produced by Black Cat Educational Software.

Books

Maths through Spreadsheets by Bryan Dye (Software Production Associates) – can be bought with a pupil's book with accompanying teachers' notes and solutions! Provides an accompanying disk with activities compatible with Microsoft Excel. There are three pupils' books which can at times be very challenging.

Databases

Subject facts

What is a database?

A database is a collection of related data organized in such a way that it is possible to extract meaningful information set against given criteria. The concept of a database has in fact been around for many years and is not a by-product of the computer age. The difference between early databases and the modern computer age database is that the former was exclusively paper-based and modern databases are electronic. We may not think of them as such, but common paper databases would include address books, telephone directories, recipe books and dictionaries.

Advantages and disadvantages of electronic databases

Advantages of an electronic database	Disadvantages of an electronic database
Can store vast amounts of data on small disks very simply	Problems of data security: data stored electronically needs to be covered by the data protection act
Far more efficient sorting, editing searching, and amending data	
Easy to assimilate large amounts of data which can be displayed in graphical form	Viruses can jeopardize a computer system
	Databases rely on accurate data entry and errors at this input stage can affect the validity of a whole project
Back-ups in case of loss or damage can be made easily	

The difference between data and information

There is often confusion about when to use the word *data* and when to use the word *information*. In everyday usage the two words have come to mean the same thing. However, in the context of work on databases, data should be considered as being that which is unprocessed: lacking structure, organization and meaning. Information, on the other hand, is processed data that has structure and organization, and thus meaning.

Parts of a database

The diagram below shows the elements that make up both a paper-based database and its digital counterpart:

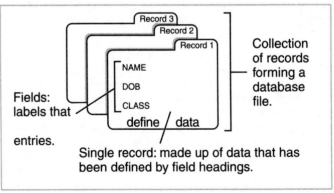

Organizing your data

Imagine going into a library where all the books had been placed on the shelves in random order, or a dictionary where word entries had been jumbled up. Finding your book or word would be extremely difficult, if not impossible.

Without organization a database would be pretty useless. A database needs to be organized in such a way that information can be located quickly and efficiently.

Characteristics of fields

Each individual field has many characteristics, some of which may be unique. These determine how data is entered, displayed and processed.

Characteristic	Description
NAME	Each field will have its own individual name that will identify the data.
SIZE	Fields are normally limited in size, so words or numerical values are not permitted to exceed a certain maximum length. Not only does this help to conserve memory but also acts as an error check. The date of birth field in the example above may have a maximum length of 10 characters that will also be linked to the format chosen: 28/07/1992.
TYPE	Fields are also divided into three broad categories which relate to the type of data being held:
	Alphanumeric – this refers to text entries
	Numeric – this refers to numerical values: amounts, prices, dates and so on. Formats for dates and times are usually pre-defined and the number of digits can be specified.
	Choice – entries are restricted to specific options, such as a yes/no question.

Stages of a database project
Establish a purpose

Setting up a database can be a very lengthy process. It involves a lot of planning and hard work so it is a good idea to make sure you have a good reason to start, a purpose and an achievable goal. See the example given in Teaching Ideas below for guidance.

Plan the database

Planning an effective database needs careful organization and foresight.

Careful thought at the planning stage will improve the efficiency of your database. It is a good idea to remind pupils of the questions and queries they are hoping to answer at the end. For example, if a database on the Tudors is to be created, what lines of enquiry are they hoping to follow? If they want the database to assimilate data on Tudor explorers or famous female Tudors, then relevant data is required. It is important to remember that the quality of assimilated information is very much linked to the quality and accuracy of the data that has been entered in the creation of the database, and as such will affect how useful the database is.

Questions to ask at the planning stage

What data needs to be collected so that my queries can be answered?
How many records do I need to collect sufficient data?
How many fields are alphanumeric and how many are numeric?
Can I offer choices to make data collection more efficient?
Can I incorporate validity checks to minimize errors at the input stage?

For example, specifying date formats may highlight typing errors if the format is not followed; limiting the length of fields means the computer will not accept entries longer or shorter than certain lengths which should correspond to correct entries. Range checks will place a limit on the entry. If age is a field to be completed by a group of Year 6 pupils, the range check will be 10–11yrs.

Capture the data

Once you have established a purpose, and planned and organized your database, it is necessary to plan and design a method of data capture. In other words, how is the actual data going to be collected? Data collection sheets in the form of questionnaires are the most common forms of data collection. These forms need to be well thought out and designed so that data collection once they have been filled in is quick and accurate. Questionnaires intended to be filled out by third parties need to be simple but well constructed and different formats should be considered for different audiences.

Useful features to include in a questionnaire:

Tick boxes:
Do you eat meat?   YES ☐   NO ☐

Multiple-choice options:
What colour eyes do you have? Please circle your answer.

  Blue   Green   Brown   Hazel

Range options:
How old are you? Please tick appropriate box.

5-7 ☐   7-11 ☐   Older ☐

Collecting factual data is relatively simple and should be fairly accurate, but pupils should be encouraged to think about reasons why people may give inaccurate replies. For example, people may lie about their age and weight if they feel embarrassed – perhaps anonymous questionnaires would help in these types of cases. Inaccuracies may occur because people are unsure of their answers, for example they may not remember how old they were when they first started to get pocket money and so may give a wild guess. Offering unlimited free choice may also prove problematic. Imagine asking people what their all-time favourite song was. Unless a large sample was taken, the results might not prove too useful as the data collected would be too disparate. Offering a choice of songs may be one way around the problem, though would not produce strictly accurate feedback to the question.

Input the raw data
Once the data has been collected, either by research or interview, it needs to be entered into the database. If the fields were well planned and keyword lists offered at appropriate points this should not prove cumbersome. See 'Useful features to include in a questionnaire' above.

Process the data
Turning data into information is only achieved through this critical stage.

What can a database do?
● Individual fields can be sorted alphabetically or numerically, in ascending or descending order. For

example, you could sort the names of all Tudor monarchs alphabetically, sort Tudor monarchs according to their date of birth, or sort according to number of children.

● Relational operators help to narrow down a search. Common relational operators are:

> *greater than*
< *less than*
= *equal to*

Using these you could now pinpoint monarchs who were married more than once, for example, or monarchs who had exactly four children.

● You can limit a search using the logical operators *and*, *or* and *not*. So, now you could pinpoint monarchs that were married *and* had two children, or monarchs who were *not* married.

Present your findings

Presenting your information in a suitable format is the next major step. The following points need to be considered:

● What information am I trying to deliver?
● Who is my audience?
● Have I got appropriate graphical representations of my information – pie charts, bar charts, scatter graphs and so on? (See the section on spreadsheets (page 79) for use of appropriate graphs and charts.)
● What package shall I use to put my presentation together – word processor, DTP? Are they compatible? Can I cut, copy and paste objects from my data-handling package?

Evaluate the database

Questions to be answered:

Did I achieve what I set out to?
Were there gaps in my database?
If I were to do this exercise again, what would I change?

Integrating ICT

The advantages of the electronic database have provided all curriculum areas with an additional source of data storage, retrieval and assimilation. Databases in maths provide a tool that makes dealing with numerical data far less of a chore, and graphical representations make more sense to pupils than abstract figures. Planning questionnaires is a good vehicle for language activities, while exploring thematic databases in history and geography adds another dimension to pupils' research skills.

Why you need to know these facts

Data handling features in many areas of the National Curriculum, not to mention direct references to it in the ICT curriculum. The Programmes of Study for both Key Stage 1 and Key Stage 2 mention the use of databases in the paragraphs dedicated to Knowledge, Skills and Understanding. The necessary skills involved are vital to empower pupils with what can be an extensive research tool.

Vocabulary

Relational database – rather than having one large database file it is often more efficient to have two or more separate but related files. For example, a school might have a pupils' details database with an additional relational database file concerned with pupils' exam results. For the two files to be linked, at least one field should be the same; the key field, in this case the obvious one is name.

Amend – to change or alter a record.

Append – to add a new record.

Legend – similar to a key used to provide a guide to charts and graphs.

Record – a collection of related fields.

Query – specifies certain conditions which the database program has to match when searching.

Match – a record which satisfies the query conditions.

Flat file database – simple one-file database structure.

Sort – to organize data in order of, for example, size or frequency.

Amazing facts

● The largest collection of genealogical data in the world is on the Internet. The Mormon Church has placed 400 million names from their records of 2 billion people in a database dating back to 1500. Take a look for yourself at www.familysearch.org.

● Holmes is the name given to the extensive database used by police forces to store data across the UK. Can you guess why?

● In 1890 the US government commissioned a gentleman by the name of Herman Hollerith to process all their census data using punch cards. The whole process took two and a half years, which was at least eight years faster than it would have taken using traditional methods. Once Hollerith realized the market for such data processing, he started a company named IBM in 1924. The rest, as they say, is history.

Information from computer databases is true and accurate.
The information gained from a database is only as good as the raw data that went in. To coin a famous phrase, 'Garbage in, garbage out'.

Avoid using the 'A–Z' approach to teaching databases. It is not always necessary or practical to create a database from scratch. Instead, focus on key aspects that address specific learning objectives, both within ICT and the subject area being taught.

Check whether you can buy ready-prepared files for the database program you are using. These are excellent for practising interrogation skills and save valuable teacher preparation time.

If you are thinking of starting a database project from scratch, it is a good idea to give pupils a valid reason to do so, encompassed within a meaningful context. The following are a few suggestions:

Mrs Drew is the headteacher of a local high school. She has been put in charge of organizing the leavers' party. However, she feels she is a little out of touch and rather than organize a disaster she has decided to use a database program to carry out an investigation and process some useful information. Can you construct a useful questionnaire that would help Mrs Drew find out the likes and dislikes of her pupils? Think about the decisions concerning food, music and entertainment Mrs Drew would need to make.

Mr Potter, the new deputy headteacher, has decided to carry out a school census in order to find out more about the pupils at his school. He has decided that the best way forward would be to collect and sort data using a database program. In small groups, decide which areas of interest need to be covered (family, sports, entertainment and so on), then think of six questions for each of these areas.

Ricky Nansbron, a pupil in Year 6 at Sunnycliffe School, has decided to approach the headmaster about opening a school tuck shop. To convince the headmaster that his plan is a good one he has to produce facts and figures. He has decided that a database program will be the best tool for his research. His aim is to produce graphs to show that pupils want a tuck shop, that they have the money to spend in a tuck shop, and some indication as to what types of items the tuck shop should sell. Produce a suitable questionnaire for data collection, carry out a small survey and produce some suitable graphs.

Branching databases

A branching database is a useful tool for sorting a group of objects. The basic idea of a branching database is to sort data using selected criteria. Questions are phrased to systematically sort a large group of objects until each object is isolated. For example:

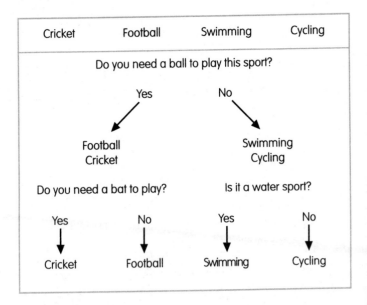

Children will need an example to help them get started. The tree diagram may be created on paper or the computer. There are also a number of commercially produced database files that pupils can use to carry out queries. Use these to prepare a list of questions for pupils to answer using the database.

Software

Suitable database programs for Key Stage 1:
Picture Point – good for simple surveys and comes with 6 topic files. Available from Longman Logotron (tel: 01223 425558).
Counter – simple to use with useful icons to help navigate.

Suitable database programs for Key Stage 2:
Clipboard – an extension to *Counter* with additional features appropriate for Key Stage 2 pupils.
Junior Pinpoint – allows the user to design and print data-collection sheets. *Pinpoint* data files are also available. From Longman Logotron (tel: 01223 425558).

Books

Finding Out – Using Reference Materials on CD-ROM, (NCET) – this resource aims to develop pupils' research skills based around their work on CD-ROM encyclopaedias. These databases are often forgotten when planning work on handling data but they can be of great help when teaching pupils important research skills.

Resources

Desktop publishing

What is it?

A desktop publishing (DTP) program is concerned with creating documents that require layouts more complex than those possible with a word processor. They commonly incorporate text, pictures and other graphic elements such as borders, boxes and word art. Whilst having the basic tools to produce such elements, these will not always be advanced. DTPs true use lies with its ability to combine elements from other packages, though it would be true to say that most educational DTP programs aim to provide a total solution to page design.

Subject facts

Working with frames.

To make page layout flexible and easy to adjust, a desktop publishing program usually works with frames – text frames and picture frames are two common examples. Once the desired content has been put into the frame it can be moved, enlarged, reduced, copied, cut, or arranged around other frames on the page.

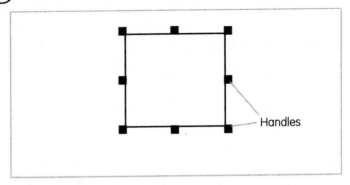

To manipulate a frame in this way it first needs to be selected. Once this is done (usually by clicking on the frame), handles will appear on the frame's border which allow the frame to be manipulated in one or more directions.

Text is moved around a page using text frames. In this way different possible layouts can be modelled with ease and efficiency. To insert a picture into a document a picture frame needs to be created. A picture is then inserted into the frame using similar methods as those used in other programs. Once again the frame may be moved around the page to model several possible layouts with ease.

Page layout

Unless a document requires a specific page layout a DTP program is not required. Simple lines of text going across the page are best achieved with a word processing package. However, designing page layouts that are more complex requires the use of a DTP program.

Text wrap

Virtually all DTP programs will support text wrapping. This is when text is wrapped around irregularly shaped objects such as pictures. Text can normally be wrapped around the frame or around the contour of the picture.

Integrating ICT

As presenting information is important in all subject areas, desktop publishing will be a vital skill for pupils to master. Report writing in particular would be best suited to a DTP program as inserting charts, graphs and pictures is made simple. Word processors on the other hand may prove a little less than flexible. Long pieces of text, though, are best produced using a standard word processor first, before being imported in to the DTP software.

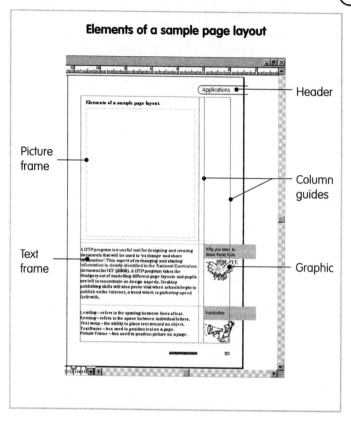

A DTP program is a useful tool for designing and creating documents that will be used to 'exchange and share information'. This aspect of exchanging and sharing information is clearly identified in the National Curriculum document for ICT (2000). A DTP program takes the drudgery out of modelling different page layouts and pupils are left to concentrate on design aspects. Desktop publishing skills will also prove vital when schools begin to publish on the Internet, a trend which is gathering speed forthwith.

Why you need to know these facts

Leading – refers to the spacing between lines of text.
Kerning – refers to the space between individual letters.
Text wrap – the ability to place text around an object.
Text frame – box used to position text on a page.
Picture frame – box used to position a picture on a page.
Word Art – Text that has been formed in to shapes.

Vocabulary

Amazing facts

● Most DTP programs allow the space between individual letters to be adjusted, known as kerning.

Golden rules

● Text that is any more than a few paragraphs in length should be produced in a word processor and then imported in to the DTP software.
● When designing a page never use more than three different fonts
● Once pupils discover the ease with which graphics can be incorporated into a document there may be a tendency to overdo this. Ask pupils to think carefully and justify their use of clip art, border art, word art and so on.

Handy tips

● Rather than adjusting individual objects which is difficult and time consuming, group objects together. This will allow you to work with the whole group as if it was one, maintaining their positions relative to each other. Check your particular DTP program to see how this is done.
● Do not allow pupils to use templates too early. Whilst they are useful at a later stage, they need to be introduced to the basics of frame creation and manipulation first.
● Use the zoom facility to home in on the frame you are working on, though when checking overall layout it is important to see the whole page.
● Always make sure pupils have a hand-sketched design they have put some thought into before attempting work on the computer. Whilst this sketch need not be detailed it will give a starting point from which pupils can model changes.
● Keep a book of sample fonts and border art that is available on the class computer for pupils to browse through and make initial selections.

Questions

Do I need any other programs apart from a DTP package to produce a document?
Strictly speaking, a DTP program should only be used to organize the various elements of your document on the page. The text should be produced using a word processor and graphics should either be scanned in or imported from a graphics program.

What should I do if I'm not sure what size I should make my text frame?

This should not be a worry at all; if your text frame is too small simply enlarge it and if it is too big reduce it. If your text runs onto another page your DTP program should have a facility that automatically creates a connecting frame. Some programs even have a facility whereby adjustments are made to the text so that it fits in the necessary space.

What is a template?

DTP programs nearly always come with a set of ready-made templates. A template for a brochure, for example, will contain all the frames and design elements ready to be personalized with the necessary information. Apart from typing in the required text and inserting graphics of your choice all other design and formatting tasks will have been done.

Apart from report writing where the DTP program is used to organize information from different sources (a graph produced using spreadsheet modelling, a word-processed report, a piece of clip art) it can also be used for many specific projects. These will all require research, preparation away from the computer, and time to model different page layouts. Together with an awareness of purpose and audience, groups of pupils working together will find the end results rewarding.

Teaching ideas

Project	Possible Context
Brochure	School brochure, or a brochure relating to a class visit, historical building, Town Hall etc.
Newspaper Adverts	Scope for a lot of language work with particular focus upon persuasive text.
Menu	This project can be given many different angles. Pupils could research a Tudor/Victorian menu, a healthy menu, or a gruesome menu whereby pupils invent their own recipes.
Letter-headed paper	Lots of language work and specific layout required, although pupils can be given the opportunity to personalize their letterhead with their own logo designed in a drawing program. If a simpler option is required a piece of clip art could be inserted instead.
Birthday Invitations	Opportunity to concentrate on purpose and audience.

Resources

Software
Talking Textease – Available from Sherston Software (tel: 01666 843200, www.sherston.com).
Microsoft Publisher – Published by Microsoft. Available from most software companies.

Multimedia authoring

Subject facts

What is multimedia authoring?
Multimedia authoring is otherwise defined as the creation of a document, often referred to as a presentation, that incorporates a number of different media, including text, sound, graphics, animation and video, all on screen.

Multimedia software
Producing such a document may at first seem like a mammoth task. However, the best software solution (and there are many of these on the market) will make it child's play. When deciding which software to buy, the following questions should be considered:
● Are page links, hot spots and buttons easy to set up?
● Does the software offer special effects, for example, page fade-outs?
● Which graphic, sound and video file formats are accepted, and are they easy to place into a presentation?
● Are pages easily linked?
● Can text be imported? Which file format should it be?
● Is frame management simple and effective?
● Is it possible to 'switch off' the editing facilities so that readers of the finished presentation are unable to make changes?
● Does the software have relevant copyright-free resources for pupils to use in their presentations?
● Does the software allow you to make a copy of your presentation on CD-ROM or floppy disk so that you can pass it on to others to view, and is it possible to run the finished presentation without the authoring software? (This can be significant when distributing the presentation.)

Hardware requirements
A multimedia presentation does not have to include all types of media, so it is not essential to have a multimedia

computer. However, to incorporate sound and video the necessary hardware will be required. Graphics and video files are also memory intensive, and your computer will need to have a sizeable hard disk to store them in any significant quantity. See the hardware chapter (page 9) for more details.

In addition to a computer, the following resources will also be useful, especially if a presentation is to incorporate full multimedia features:

animation software
scanner
digital camera
music software
Clip Art and sound files (copyright-free)
graphics software (to produce and manipulate pictures).

Stages involved in the creation of a multimedia presentation

A successful multimedia presentation calls for a high level of planning. It will be easier if you break it down into the following stages:

● Select a theme for the presentation (some are listed below).

● Hold a class brainstorm on themes for pages, ideas for pictures, animations; talk about the proposed audience and their particular needs.

● Plan an overview of the presentation: how many pages in total, outline contents for each page, list of resources required (Clip Art, sound files).

● Sketch out rough page layouts (a storyboard is helpful) and indicate links.

● In small groups, ask pupils to design individual page layouts, indicating all the features that need to be included.

● Assign pupils their specific tasks.

● Carry out research and collect relevant materials; for example, research and word-process text, take necessary photographs, scan and edit final images for the page.

● Create the presentation (incorporate individual assignments on final page layout).

● Check and debug the presentation: run through the presentation noting any errors which need to be corrected; check links, hot spots and buttons.

● Save the finished presentation on a floppy disk or CD-ROM.

● Distribute the presentation to appropriate recipients.

Buttons

A button is very much like a switch and is used to activate a procedure. Buttons can be visible, invisible, represented by a picture or text.

Buttons should only be used when there is a specific purpose. Use a button icon to:

turn pages backward and forward
show pictures
play a sound
start an animation or video clip
jump to links.

Text

Whilst text is necessary for conveying important information, a multimedia presentation should not contain text alone. Text should be as brief as possible and attractively presented. Care should be taken when choosing fonts and colours, making sure that the overall effect is pleasing and effective. Stick to one or two fonts and give a degree of consistency to the presentation.

Sounds

Sounds can be very effective in adding atmosphere, interest and excitement to a page. Sound files can take the form of sound effects, dialogue and music, and can be assigned to buttons or hotspots, transforming a very normal page of text into one which is full of interest.

Pictures

A multimedia presentation should at the very least contain text and graphics. Hand-drawn pictures can easily be scanned into a document whilst photographs can be incorporated using a digital camera or film developed onto Photo-CD. If you do not have access to either of these, prints could be scanned for use in the presentation. It is useful to note, however, that scanned images are usually fairly large and keeping them as small as possible is one way to conserve valuable disk space. Selecting file formats that economize on disk space would be another useful point to remember; JPEG files, for example, are far more economical than bitmap files.

Copyright permitting, pictures can also be cut and pasted from CD-ROMs. Simply find the picture on the relevant CD-ROM and press the PRINT SCREEN button on your keyboard. This will capture the screen image and place it on the clipboard. Now open Paintbrush or Paint, depending on which version of Windows you have, and paste the image onto the canvas. Use the cropping tools to edit the picture and save the image as normal.

Animation
For pupils to create their own animations by hand takes a lot of time and expertise. Animation packages are now widely available and these make animation a practical classroom activity. Some multimedia authoring packages such as Adobe *Illuminatus* have an animation effect tool which gives the effect of animation by showing a selection of pictures in quick succession.

Video
Just as a sound card is required to add sound to a presentation, a video card is required to add a video clip, along with the necessary software. Even a very short video clip takes up a considerable amount of disk space, and put together with the fact that reproduction of the video clip requires a powerful multimedia computer, it may be wise to think carefully about its inclusion.

Gone are the days when the noisiest thing about the classroom computer was its squeaking trolley or the 9-pin dot matrix printer that was linked to it. Computers today are multimedia machines that stimulate more than one sense and which empower the user to take charge of his/her discovery path. Electronic text, sound, graphics, video and animations have changed dramatically the role of the reader. Far from taking a submissive role, the reader becomes very much a proactive participant. The non-linear nature of the text gives the reader the right to make decisions as to where to go next and whether to follow a link now or later. To be able to create such a multimedia experience for another reader and be aware of all its elements and implications must surely be a step pupils need to take to enrich their learning potential.

Why you need to know these facts

A multimedia presentation has to include all types of media, including sound, text, pictures, graphics, video and animations.
A multimedia presentation need only have content appropriate to its subject matter. As long as there is more than just text to a presentation, it can be classed as being multimedia.

Common misconceptions

Golden rules

- Always check the copyright status of a picture, text extract, video or sound file which has not been created by yourself. See the Resources section for contact details about copyright information.
- When creating pictures in a drawing package, make sure the size of the canvas is no bigger than it need be. This will ensure the graphic file will be as small as possible.

Handy tips

- Use the guided tours which many software packages offer to introduce the concepts of multimedia authoring to pupils.
- If your computer has a sound card and a microphone, together with a small application that comes free with Windows called Sound Recorder, it is possible to create your own sounds very easily. However, the sound files produced in this way will be .wav files which tend to produce large file sizes.
- Keep video clips short. Video files take up vast amounts of memory and require high-performance computers to show them effectively.
- The safest format to save text for importation is plain text format (.txt).

Teaching ideas

True and False Quiz

It's possible to create a multimedia quiz without any multimedia authoring software. In fact, for the following project you will only need a simple word processor like WordPad and two programs that come with Windows called Sound Recorder and Object Packager:

- Open WordPad and type one 'true' fact based around an appropriate theme. For example:

> The Polar bear lives in the Arctic.

- Create a sound file for the 'true' response. Open Sound Recorder (if you have it, you will find it in the *Accessories > Multimedia* menus). Using a microphone, record the phrase 'Well done' and save using the file name welldone.wav
- Create a graphic that will be used to activate sound when clicked on. Open Paint and draw a small symbol with the word *True* underneath it. Select your picture and click on *Copy* from the *Edit* menu.
- Link the sound with a graphic. Open Object Packager (if you have difficulty finding this program, use the *Find File*

utility in the *Start m*enu). Click on *File* and then *Import*. Select welldone.wav to import the sound. Click on the word *Appearance*. Now choose *Paste* from the *Edit* menu. Your graphic should now appear in the left-hand window. Now select *Copy Package* from the *Edit* menu. The sound and graphic are now linked together and stored on the clipboard.

● Return to WordPad and position the cursor underneath the question to one side. Select *Paste* from the *Edit* menu. Repeat the above but this time create a 'false' graphic and a sound file with the phrase 'Bad luck' linked to it. Paste this new packaged sound and graphic file underneath the question next to the first one.

Repeat this process for more questions to complete the test, remembering that not all will be true statements, and that if a statement is false, the false symbol will need the 'Well done' sound file attached to it. Save the word processed file and, when run, you will have a multimedia quiz:

> The polar bear lives in the Arctic.
> False   True

When clicked, the appropriate sound file will be played.

Software

Illuminatus – multimedia software available from Research Machines (tel: 01235 826000, www.rm.com).
Multimedia Textease – an extension of the popular word processor, produced by Softease.
HyperStudio – multimedia authoring software available from Broderbund.
Flying Colours – painting and drawing software with lots of effects and tools for creating and manipulating images. Available from Longman Logotron (tel: 01223 425558).
Treasure Chest – a collection of curriculum based, copyright-free pictures, photographs, symbols and sound effects. Produced by SEMERC (tel: 0161 827 2527).

Useful addresses
Information about copyright may be obtained from the following organizations:
Copyright Licensing Agency, 90 Tottenham Court Rd, London W1P 9HE (tel: 020 7436 5931).
Design & Artists' Copyright Society, St Mary's Clergy House, Whitechurch Lane, London E1 7QR (020 7336 8811)

Graphics

Digital art is all around us – in advertising, films and
television – and whilst it grows ever more sophisticated,
simple-to-use packages are available with user-friendly
graphical interfaces that make working with a computer a
non-technical task and which can support the most gifted
and the most challenged artist alike.

Bitmap versus vector

Digital images are created in one of two ways: as bitmapped
images or as vector images. A bitmapped image is made up
of individual dots (pixels) on the screen; a vector image is
made up of separate objects and flat or fading colours: lines,
ovals, rectangles and so on.

A comparison between bitmap and vector images

Bitmap	Vector
Image created by pixels, sometimes called raster graphics, good for detailed work	Image created by separate objects created using geometric shapes, often called object-orientated graphics
Images require large amounts of memory	Require less memory than bitmapped images
Are not as easily or efficiently manipulated	More flexible and can be re-sized and stretched with ease
Become ragged at the edges when enlarged	Keep their definition whether enlarged or reduced

Software

Software can be split into two distinct groups: drawing
packages and image-manipulation software. The former
deals largely with creating digital pictures whilst the latter
specializes in altering existing images using a variety of
tools. In reality, a drawing package will also have a limited
capability for manipulation just as an image-manipulation
program will have a limited capability for drawing.

Common drawing tools

There are vast numbers of drawing programs available on
the market but most will offer similar types of drawing
tools. The toolbar below is that of *Adobe Photoshop*, a
professional drawing package, although many of the tools
and their icons are similar in Windows' Paint which comes
as standard with Windows 95/98.

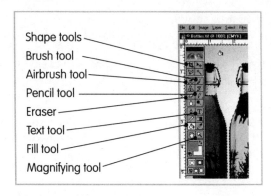

Shape tools
Brush tool
Airbrush tool
Pencil tool
Eraser
Text tool
Fill tool
Magnifying tool

The Bezier curve

Most drawing programs support Bezier curves. Once mastered, the Bezier curve is perhaps the most useful drawing tool available.

A basic Bezier curve is made up of two end points called anchor points and multiple points (called nodes) along the line that are used to define the shape of the curve. These are used to manipulate the curve, turning a simple curve into virtually any shape desired.

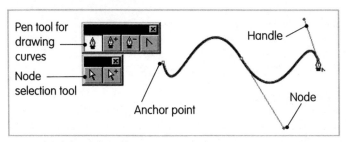

Pen tool for drawing curves

Node selection tool

Handle

Node

Anchor point

Metamorphosing (morphing)

This technique gradually turns one image into another. It is often done using images of two people. Many software packages now include this feature, and it can be a lot of fun creating interesting effects.

Rotating and flipping

Objects can be rotated through any number of degrees in most drawing packages by grabbing an object and rotating it manually with the mouse. The default pivot point is usually at the centre, but some programs allow the user to alter this setting. Apart from rotating the object manually it is also possible to indicate a specific rotation by stating the exact rotation in degrees. Objects can also be flipped horizontally or vertically, as if reflecting them in a mirror.

Stretching and skewing

Another way to change the appearance of an object is to stretch it, vertically or horizontally, or to skew it, which basically involves stretching two opposite corners of the object, giving a 3-D effect.

Clip Art

Many programs come with a set of ready-made pictures, called Clip Art, which you can drop into documents with ease. Many Clip Art libraries are available already indexed and conveniently stored on CD-ROMs. There are also sites on the Internet that offer free items of Clip Art, and subscription websites exist where fees are charged for accessing and downloading images.

If you are working with Windows-compatible software, producing and transporting graphic images is a fairly simple task. Cut and paste techniques can add graphics to your documents with ease.

If you wish to incorporate a Clip Art image or other graphic file into a document, you will need to use the *Insert* technique. Most programs will allow you to insert graphs, charts, sound, video and graphic images to your document. The most important thing to know in this case is where the file is stored. If using a Windows program, select the *Insert* option and select *Picture*, then *From File*. You are now given the opportunity to select your file from its source and to insert the graphic in to your document.

Integrating ICT

Modern graphics packages provide many opportunities for integrating graphics work into other subject areas. Apart from the obvious links to art, where pupils are able to experiment with different techniques, there is also tremendous scope for mathematical work. Considering that computer graphics are essentially based on mathematical principles, this should not come as a surprise. Exploring the properties of different shapes, the effects of symmetry, rotation and scale are all topics that can be explored using a fairly basic art package. Exploring the effects and uses of graphics in the media, including newspapers, advertising campaigns and websites also provides a stimulating context for computer graphics work. Simple modelling activities where pupils investigate the use of different colour schemes could also be successfully incorporated at both Key Stage 1 and Key Stage 2. Armed with basic computer drawing skills, pupils can create simple floor plans and maps in geography. Older pupils can begin to explore the appropriateness of different graphics solutions, the use of scanners and digital cameras for incorporating non-computer generated art work, Clip Art, and graphics found on the Internet and on CD-ROMs.

From simple word-processed stories to multimedia presentations and web pages, graphics will always play an important role. Pupils need to grasp the basic techniques of drawing with paint packages and also how to manipulate and incorporate graphics into their work from a variety of sources.

Zipped file – a compressed file.
Compression – reducing the size of a file.
Archive – a graphic file that is stored in its compressed state.
Pixel – smallest point in an image.
Morphing – when one image gradually turns into another.
Line art – an image only made up of lines, without shading.
Crop – to cut off unwanted parts of a picture.
Thumbnail – postage stamp sized image.
Autotracing – the process of converting a bitmap image into a vector image.
Grey scale – producing a picture using shades of grey, rather than black and white or colour images.
Acronyms
CAD – Computer Aided Design.
OLE – Object Linking and Embedding.

● Even vector images are translated into bitmaps at the printing stage. This is because most printers are raster devices (that is, they deal with bitmaps). Even professional PostScript printers that use vector graphics have raster image processors that perform the translation within the printer.

● Whenever you download a picture from the Internet, make sure that you are acting legally. A lot of pictures are only free for personal or non-profit uses. If this is the case, make sure you do not publish them in a magazine that will be for sale. There are many copyright-free websites available, see the Resources section for some sources of free images.

Handy tips

- To draw a perfect square or circle using the rectangle and ellipse tools in Paint, hold down the SHIFT key.
- When you download pictures from the Internet, place them into a newly created folder so that they are easily located when you need them.
- If a black and white printer is the only one available to you, opt to have a black and white palette. This will give you shades of grey that will prove more effective when printed. In Paint choose *Attributes* from the *Image* menu and select *Black and White*.
- To enlarge or reduce the size of an image, use the scaling tool. This will change the scale of the image whilst preserving image quality.

Questions

Once an image has been compressed into a JPEG image, can it be turned back to its original file format?
No, once compressed into a JPEG file, there is no turning back. The best thing to do is to make a copy of the original.

What is the best way to store graphic images?
This depends on a number of factors. As graphic images take up a lot of space, many people compress them. However, compression is accompanied by a loss in image quality. The best option is either to compress images by the minimum possible amount (which will considerably reduce the file size without too much loss in quality), or to store images on a portable storage device such as a CD-R. CDs are coming down in price and making this latter option feasible.

Why does a bitmapped image take up more memory than a vector image?
Each dot (or pixel) that makes up a bitmap image requires computer memory. For black and white pictures, each pixel will only need one bit of memory. However, for any colour other than black or white, each pixel requires more than one bit of memory – more bits per pixel equals more colours and shades of colours. In this way a picture can very quickly become memory hungry. A vector image stores shapes instead, so requires only the type of shape, its dimensions and colour to be stored, thus saving on memory.

What is the difference between object linking and object embedding?
When you link an object to a document, any changes made to the object in its original application will automatically be

updated in the destination document. Object embedding will not update changes made in this way.

What is the difference between inserting an image by selecting Picture from the Insert menu, instead of selecting Object from the Insert menu?
Inserting an image as an object allows you to edit the image using the application that created it. To do this, simply double-click on the image.

How can I incorporate pictures drawn by pupils into a DTP package?
The only way to do this is to use a scanner. Scanning pictures in this way creates digital copies of the pictures that can be manipulated by the computer. Once the file is created and stored on your hard disk it can be inserted in the usual way.

T-shirts using computer graphics

Teaching ideas

This is a simple but effective project to make a personalized T-shirt. The project requires a few necessary resources: a simple art package which has a flip tool, an inkjet printer, and special transfer paper which needs to be compatible with your specific printer (available from most computer shops). You will also need an appropriate number of white cotton T-shirts.
● Pupils need to create a design for their T-shirt. Designs can be free choice or created around a specific theme.
● Flip your design horizontally (as if in a mirror) so that writing in particular will be the correct way round when printed on to the T-shirt.
● Print the design following the instructions for the transfer paper.
● Iron the design onto the T-shirt.

Illuminated letters using *Paint*
Using the text tool type one letter onto the canvas, enlarge the letter to the desired size and, using the other drawing tools, add effects to personalize the letter. This can then be inserted in to, for example, a word-processed story.

Spot the difference
Create a simple picture in a drawing package and save it as picture1. Copy and paste it to your DTP program, then return to picture1 and make 10 subtle changes. Re-save the picture as picture2, copy and paste this second picture next

to or under the original picture. Add title and instructions, print out and ask pupils to spot the differences.

Flip book

Simple computer animations are made from a series of individual pictures known as frames. Each frame will differ slightly from the previous one so that when the frames are shown in quick succession, they appear to be moving. The principle is exactly the same as that which is behind the old-fashioned flip book. Computer graphics, however, make the whole process far more accurate and speedy. The following is a class project whereby each member of the class produces at least one of the pictures for the flip book.

A theme for the flip book needs to be chosen; possible ones include a person running, winking, bouncing a ball, or blowing up a balloon which explodes at the end.

The first pupil (perhaps one of the better computer artists, as the first picture requires the most work) draws the first picture, saves it as picture1 and prints out two copies.

One copy is stuck on the first page of the flip book and the second is given to the second pupil, who decides on the changes for the next frame. Once these have been checked with the teacher (look out for abrupt changes; they need to be gradual), the second pupil reloads the first picture, makes the changes and re-saves it as picture2. Once again two copies of the picture are printed. The process is repeated until all the class have created a picture and the flip book is complete.

Spot the anomaly

The following activity involves the use of a scanner and lots of imagination. The age-old saying that 'the camera never lies' is repeatedly being challenged by new technologies. Any image can now be manipulated with little effort. The following activity can be changed to fit in with any historical study, though the example centres on the Victorians.

Find or scan a family portrait of Queen Victoria, and save it to the hard disk. Now scan a picture of a non-Victorian. This may be a contemporary, such as the Prime Minister, the headteacher or a person from another era, such as Henry VIII. Using appropriate manipulation software, edit the original picture so it includes the anomaly and print it out. Allow pupils to come up with other ideas – a picture of a Victorian classroom with a computer in the corner, a picture of a Victorian kitchen with a washing machine, a picture of a Victorian grocer's shop showing a pizza for sale – the possibilities are endless.

Software

Tom Paint – a great starting point for early years and Key Stage 1 pupils. Available from Ransom Publishing (tel: 01491 613711, www.ransompublishing.co.uk).
Dazzle Plus – the ability to customize the toolbar makes this a good choice for both younger and more experienced users. Available from SEMERC (tel: 0161 827 2527).
Sherston Primary Curriculum Clip Art – contains over 2300 images categorized by subject (with descriptive text). Many images are available in both colour and black and white. With a useful browser facility and a free site licence, this is one of the better Clip Art choices for primary schools. From Sherston Software (tel: 01666 843200, www.sherston.com).

Resources

Monitoring and sensing

Monitoring in modern life

Monitoring is as much part of our everyday lives as any other common convenience. From complex monitoring machines in hospitals to petrol pumps, monitoring is a fact of everyday life. In fact, such dependence on these computerized activities was partly the cause of the millennium bug panic.

Subject facts

The necessary hardware

Hardware and software solutions to monitoring in schools are gradually improving and manufacturers have become wise to the fact that offering suitable hardware is not all that is required. Data logging and monitoring solutions have therefore recognized the need for support materials, and packs now come together with the necessary hardware, software and support materials for both teachers and pupils.

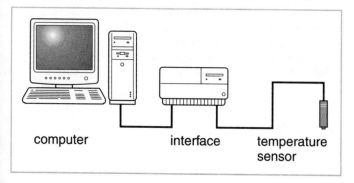

computer   interface   temperature sensor

Sensors

A sensor is a monitoring device that measures a physical change in the environment. It is linked to a computer to which it sends its data for interpretation. Sensors can be digital or analogue devices, though the latter requires an analogue to digital converter in order to communicate with the computer. The most common types of sensors used in classrooms are those which detect and monitor light, sound, pressure, acidity, and temperature.

Interface

The most expensive piece of equipment required to carry out monitoring activities is the interface box. This is the link between the sensor and the computer which is used to feed back data collected.

Why do data logging?

- Pupils are able to concentrate on investigative skills.
- It provides an excellent medium for pupils to study the practical use of ICT in the world around them.
- It supports and extends pupils' scientific and technological understanding.
- It enables pupils to investigate activities that would otherwise have been difficult or impractical.
- Investigations can be repeated with ease if inaccuracies are suspected.

Stages involved in a scientific data-logging activity

- Identify investigation
- encourage pupils to make a hypothesis that can be tested
- select appropriate sensors and equipment
- set up equipment and investigation, paying attention to control variables in order to establish a fair test
- establish the period of data logging and time intervals to be used (these will be dependent on task and software limitations)
- decide how results are to be displayed: printout, a changing screen display, or graph
- start data logging
- analyse data
- draw up conclusions.

Factors to consider when buying data-logging equipment

- How many sensors come with the kit, are they appropriate and will additional ones need to be purchased?
- Is the hardware sturdy and up to the rigours of primary

use? This is particularly pertinent when purchasing portable kits for outside use.
● Is compatible software included? If not, which software is best?
● Check portable kits for battery life and memory capacity.

Integrating ICT

Monitoring and sensing activities will be of greatest use in the science curriculum. Pupils will be able to concentrate on investigative skills as opposed to being preoccupied with the mechanics of collecting and recording results (unless the objectives of the lesson state the acquisition and development of such skills). Pupils' learning can be focused and time can be spent on analysis and interpretation of results. Too often science lessons stop at the end of an investigation because the efforts involved in completing the practicalities are so great and pupils run out of time or energy for the fundamental learning that should be taking place afterwards.

The Programme of Study for ICT specifically states the requirement for Key Stage 2 pupils to 'monitor events and respond to them' (ICT 2b). Furthermore, the successful integration of ICT with regard to science can only take place with knowledge of monitoring and sensing. Teachers and pupils need to get to grips with the necessary skills required to use the hardware involved, and only then can they work towards meaningful learning experiences, which the successful integration of ICT aims to promote. Getting to this stage is, however, easier said than done, which explains why many schools are having difficulty with this area. Initial setting-up costs are quite high, both in terms of specialist equipment and time. The benefits, however, are there to be had and schools have an obligation to provide these to their pupils.

Why you need to know these facts

Interface – a device used to connect two separate pieces of equipment together.
Sensor – a monitoring device that measures physical changes and sends corresponding data back to the processor, usually via an interface.
Time interval – time between individual readings when data logging.
Data logging – using a computer to automatically measure variables such as light, sound and heat.

Vocabulary

Amazing facts

A computer scientist living in the Canadian Rocky Mountains has devised a system whereby the temperature inside his house remains at a constant 22.513 degrees Celsius. It is so precisely monitored that it reacts to body heat so that when a person walks into or leaves a room, adjustments will be made.

Golden rules

Always familiarize yourself with new hardware and software before you unleash it in the classroom. The frustrations of a wasted lesson due to equipment failure (or the failure to be able to use the equipment properly) are not worth it.

Handy tips

● Have a long-term buying strategy and build up a set of compatible hardware and software.
● Invest in high-quality sensors, as cheaper ones won't last or cope with the rigours of classroom life.
● Ask for a demonstration of the equipment before you buy and incorporate it into a staff meeting where everyone can get a look.

Questions

Do different data-logging kits require different types of software?
Some do, and you will find these come packaged with their own software. However, *Insight 2* and *Junior Insight* from Logotron are compatible with many programs and are fast becoming a standard in schools. When purchasing the software, you will need to specify the format you require, PC or Acorn for example.

What is remote data logging?
This is when data is logged away from the computer using a portable data-logging kit. Data is then transferred to the computer for analysis at a later time.

What's the difference between a digital sensor and an analogue sensor?
A simple digital sensor records a binary 1 for an 'on' position or a binary 0 for an 'off' position. A pressure pad would be a good example of a digital sensor. As soon as someone steps on the pressure pad it would be 'on' and as soon as they step off it, it would be 'off'. An analogue sensor,

on the other hand, will give a varying value. A temperature sensor would be one example. For the processor to deal with analogue feedback, an analogue to digital converter is needed.

The following are suggestions for investigations that could be carried out using data-logging equipment:

Does size of cup affect time taken for tea to cool down?
How quiet is the library compared to the classroom?
When is the coldest part of the day?
Which brand of crisp is the noisiest to eat?
I like my coffee very hot. Shall I put the milk in before the hot water or after?
Heating costs are too high. When is the earliest possible time the heating could be switched off in school?

Hardware
LogIT DataMeter 1000 – allows you to log with or without your computer and its built-in screen means that it's equally capable of data logging live or remotely. Available from Longman Logotron (tel: 01223 425558).

Software
Junior Insight – required software to data log with LogIT meters and interfaces. Availabe as above.

Modelling

What is a computer model?
Computer modelling encompasses a vast array of activities. In non-computing terms, the word *model* is used to describe a physical imitation of an object. Computer modelling, however, adds a further dimension, and will attempt to imitate an object's behaviour. Indeed, a computer model will often, as is the case with spreadsheet modelling, attempt to imitate a real-life situation. Straight away we come to realize that the computer model is much more than just an alternative method or a simple reconstruction – computer modelling should be a problem-solving activity, instigated by a problem, driven by an hypothesis and, where possible, proven by a rule.

Why model?

Using a computer model, pupils are given the opportunity to experience at second hand events that they couldn't in real life because they are too dangerous, too expensive, physically or geographically impossible, or otherwise impractical.

Being able to experience scenarios which they would otherwise not have been able to gives pupils an opportunity to at least begin to explore a model's behaviour and their reactions to it. For example, an adventure game can be a great starting point for pupils to extend and practise their problem-solving capabilities. Teamwork, being able to get on with others and to delegate responsibilities based on personal strengths and weaknesses are skills which pupils can develop and gain greatly from.

Processes involved in modelling activities
- Pupils become decision makers.
- Pupils can easily control and change variables in their experiments.
- Pupils are able to see the outcomes of their decisions quickly.
- Pupils use their learning to predict outcomes.
- Pupils are able to make and test hypotheses.

Advantages of computer modelling

A computer model provides pupils with the opportunity to experience events that they would otherwise not have access to, encouraging and extending problem-solving skills and lateral thinking. Using a model allows for easy 'What if...?' testing, where changes can be made instantly, allowing pupils to make predictions and test hypotheses, identify patterns and relationships and define rules in a collaborative environment.

Integrating ICT

There are opportunities to use computer modelling in nearly all areas of the primary curriculum. Simulation-type adventure games can be found based around many different themes. Specific simulations that aim to provide a computer alternative to an activity can also prove useful to the over-burdened teacher. Simulating electrical circuits at the computer, for example, could prove beneficial for reinforcement of a topic, especially if resources are limited. Mathematical modelling, using formulae in spreadsheets to answer 'What if...?' questions, and Logo is very useful at extending pupils' learning.

The National Curriculum document for ICT makes direct references for the inclusion of computer modelling. Whilst Key Stage 1 concentrates more on the exploration of simulations, the need at Key Stage 2 to progress further is evident. In order for pupils to achieve Levels 3 and 4 at Key Stage 2, they need to take a far more investigative approach: pupils will need to investigate the effects of changing variables, hypothesize, and detect patterns and relationships in their findings.

Why you need to know these facts

The rescue of 103 hostages taken prisoner by pro-Palestinian guerrillas in 1976 was only achieved after the Israeli soldiers that executed the whole operation had simulated the operation on a mock-up of Entebbe Airport. The success of the project impressed the American military so much that it approached ARPA (Advanced Research Projects) to investigate ways to mimic the training techniques of the Israelis electronically.

Amazing facts

Always group pupils for modelling activities. This encourages collaborative work and supports those pupils who may find modelling activities difficult.

Golden rules

● If introducing a new simulation program, do so in manageable stages. Often simulation games are based on a mission-type activity which is encompassed within an imaginary storyboard. Give pupils a précis of the story before they even get to the computer. This way characters and settings will have instant meaning.
● Take the usual precautions when deciding on working groups, considering the group dynamics of combining different personalities.

Handy tips

You need specialist software packages to carry out simulations.
Simulation games are often categorized wrongly as being adventure games. In fact this is only one type of simulation. Pupils could quite easily simulate other situations simply by using a spreadsheet, database or DTP package. A business

Common misconceptions

scenario needs only a spreadsheet program to model activities, a newsroom could be simulated by using a desktop publishing package together with perhaps the use of the Internet. The list is as exhaustive as a person's imagination and pupils can be very creative if given the opportunity.

Questions

What is a 'What if...?' scenario?

A 'What if...?' scenario is often used with mathematical activities. For example, a spreadsheet could be used to model the following scenarios:

- What if demand for hot dogs went down by 10%?
- What if I saved £2.50 each week for 12 weeks?

Both questions could quite easily be modelled using a spreadsheet. However, older pupils would need to assimilate other possible variables. If demand for hot dogs went down by 10%, could the business still make a profit? Would prices need to be increased? How could profitability be maintained: cheaper bread or hotdogs?

Teaching ideas

Simulation collage

A guided discussion about the real-life uses of simulations should form the basis of this lesson. Simulations are useful for trainee pilots, astronauts, architects, scientists, and manufacturers testing for – among other things – safety (seat belts, for example). Collages can be created using pictures, photographs or hand-drawn sketches.

Logo windmills

The following activity aims to encourage pupils to think logically and make simple predictions based on mathematical concepts they have tried and tested. Pupils should first be asked to create a basic shape that will be repeated to make the windmill effect. They need to create a procedure for this shape and name it windmill.

> Possible solutions:
> *repeat 36 [windmill rt 10]*
> *repeat 10 [windmill rt 36]*

Pupils now need to predict and then model the number of times the above shape needs to be rotated and re-drawn in order to complete a 360 degree turn.

Is there a relationship between the angle of rotation and the number of times the shape needs to be re-drawn? What other effects can be created?

Graphic models

Modelling using graphics packages is a useful and very accessible activity. One of the biggest advantages of a computer graphics package is the ability to model different colours and effects with ease and without the need to re-draw. In this way even very young pupils are able to carry out simple modelling activities.

The following activity, however, uses pupils' knowledge of a basic graphics package to model different layouts for the school playground. Pupils will first need to decide which tools they will use to represent different objects.

Introduce the problem: that the playground is to be re-modelled and new equipment needs to be positioned. Give a list of new equipment and ask the children to model at least two different possible layouts. Reasons for their final choices need to be discussed, ready for a plenary.

Spreadsheet models
Increasing profits

Pupils need to be given a spreadsheet with the following information:

Product	Number sold	Price	Income	Profit (10% of income)
Pens	750	£0.23	£172.50	£17.25
Rulers	560	£0.25	£140.00	£14.00
Rubbers	875	£0.20	£175.00	£17.50

What would happen if prices were increased by 1p?
(For each 1p price increase sales decrease by 10.)
What would happen if prices were decreased by 1p?
(For each 1p price decrease sales increase by 20.)

The above activity can be used by pupils who need a little structure for their modelling activities. Remember that the income and profit columns will need to have formulae entered in order for the model to work; these could be supplied to children in need of more support. The model has been set up and pupils are being directed about which variables to change. To extend the activity, pupils could be given greater freedom to experiment and investigate different options.

Software

Logo – many different versions of Logo exist which differ in small ways from each other. Visit Longman Logotron's website for more information at www.logo.com.

Hot Dog Stand: The Works – a simulation game where pupils are presented with the challenge of running their own business. Available from TAG Developments (tel: 01474 357350, www.tagdev.co.uk).

Simple Circuits – let pupils investigate their knowledge of circuits on screen without the hassle of fused bulbs. Available from Soft Teach (tel: 01985 840329, www.soft-teach.co.uk).

Pond Life 3-D – excellent resource for Key Stage 2 pupils who are able to create and manage their very own pond ecosystem.

Control

Subject facts

What is control technology?

Control technology involves programming computers to control devices. A burglar alarm, for instance, could be triggered when a light or a pressure sensor is activated. Automatic doors could open when a person steps onto the pressure pad that leads up to it. Modern washing machines are able to sense the weight of the load and the absorbency of the clothes and use this information to calculate the amount of water that is required. In the classroom, pupils can control devices such as turtles and create working models for themselves. All of these events are part of control technology, but for them to take place computers need to be programmed to follow a set of very specific instructions.

Making a start

With a simple control box, the correct software and a model to control, pupils can create and design their own control projects.

Typical control programming could be used to switch the lighthouse's light on for 2 seconds and then off for 2 seconds, on for 2 seconds and then off for 2 seconds for a set period of time. The number 1 in the diagram above indicates the port used on the control box that is to be switched on.

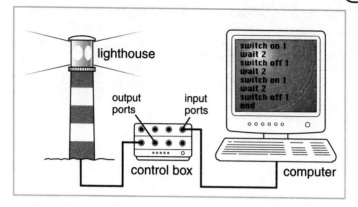

The above model has only one output, which controls the lighthouse's light. The amount of times it is switched on and off and the duration of each is dictated very precisely by the program that has been created using compatible software. Variations to the program could involve altering the number of times the light was switched on and off, or changing the duration.

Sensing and reacting

The control model above is a simple one which is responding only to the control program. A step forward would be to create a model and program a condition which needs to be met before a resulting action is activated.

Creating a night light that comes on as soon as it is dark

A model is built representing the front door of a house. A night light is also constructed. The light from the night light is connected to the buffer box using one of the output ports. A light sensor is positioned at the side of the house and is connected to one of the input ports. A program is now written to activate the light when it becomes dark.

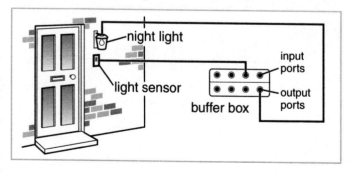

The program needs to turn the night light on as soon as it becomes dark and off as soon as it becomes light. The light sensor will instruct the computer when this occurs. The program will look something like the following:

Wait until switch 3=off	*light sensor is plugged into input 3*
Switch on 4	*bulb is plugged into output 4*
Wait until switch 3=on	
Switch off 4	
end	

Programming

Whilst computers can carry out extremely complex tasks, they are not thinking machines. A computer will only be able to carry out a control task if it is told exactly what to do, when to do it, how long to do it for and when to stop doing it! The advantages of computers being able to do such tasks, though, are many. Despite their awesome computing power, a computer never becomes bored, only occasionally feels unwell and is extremely obedient.

Roamers

A lot of control work at Key Stage 1 is done using a roamer. The Roamer is a small, simple programmable robot which not only introduces younger pupils to computer control but also to simple programming.

Logo

By Key Stage 2, pupils should be able to develop their programming skills using a programming language called Logo. Whilst there are many versions of Logo which may present slight variations in syntax, the objective is the same: to develop computer programming skills through turtle graphics.

Developing programs to draw a square using Logo

Program to draw a square using basic commands

fd 80	*80 determines the length.*
rt 90	*rt determines rotational turn,*
fd 80	*in this case 90 degrees right.*
rt 90	
fd 80	
rt 90	
fd 80	
rt 90	

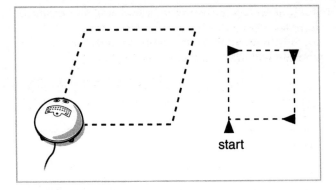

start

Increase efficiency

To increase efficiency when writing the program, it would be better to use the repeat command:

Repeat 4 [fd 80 rt 90]

By using the repeat command, the program has been simplified and economy in this way leads to fewer errors and more efficient programming.

Procedures

Wouldn't it be nice to be able to type the word 'square' and have a square appear on screen? At this point you're ready to create your own procedure. To do this you need to enter the editing box. This can be done in the following way using RM logo.

to square (this will take you to the editing box in RM Logo)
repeat 4[fd 80 rt 90]
end

What this has done is to create a procedure called 'square' which will draw a square. Once created, the only thing that needs to be typed is the command 'square'.

Variables

The only thing pupils would need to remember is that the above procedure will only draw a square with sides that are 80 logo units. This limits the usefulness of the procedure and a more flexible program is required. Pupils may suggest creating many procedures for different sized squares, and while this would be a possible solution, it would involve a great deal of programming. Pupils need to be reminded that economy and efficiency are two very important principles in computer programming.

In fact the answer lies with the introduction of variables. Once this is done, the desired dimension for the square need only to be added to the command line.
At the edit box, type:

to 'square 'side	*The program is not specifying a*
repeat 4 [fd :side rt 90]	*length*
end	

At the screen pupils are given the flexibility to draw squares of any size.

Square 60	*This number now indicates the required size of the square on this occasion.*

Advantages of teaching pupils computer programming using Logo

Develops younger pupils' skills of sequencing.
Develops precision when framing sets of instructions.
Develops an awareness of efficiency and economy – for the computer programmer, less is most definitely more.
Develops logical and accurate thought processes.
Develops problem-solving strategies.
Encourages investigative and collaborative work.
Encourages independent learning.

Integrating ICT

Control activities are useful in many areas of the curriculum. Roamer and Logo activities are particularly good at developing maths and language concepts. The Roamer is an extremely versatile device that can be used to model many different scenarios. It can even be dressed up as characters in a story! Specific control projects have an obvious and direct link with technology projects and art.

Opportunities to group pupils with different capabilities should also not be ignored. Both creative and logical thinkers have parts to play and by supporting each other, pupils are learning to work together efficiently with a respect for each individual's contribution.

Why you need to know these facts

Control technology and the processes it involves not only encourages pupils to think about the pervasive nature of computers in society but also encourages learning strategies that are sometimes under-developed in other areas of the curriculum. Pupils are encouraged to experiment, investigate and hypothesize, to correct mistakes and to think laterally when problem solving. They are given the opportunity to be creative and work in a dynamic environment where feedback is often instant.

The Roamer is only appropriate at Key Stage 1.
The Roamer can in fact be used throughout Key Stages 1 and 2 alongside Logo. At Key Stage 2, teachers may wish to link the Roamer to the computer and allow pupils to control it by writing commands in Logo.

Logo only develops mathematics and programming skills.
Logo is, first and foremost, a language and as such is a good vehicle to extend and explore this area. Conditionals such as *if*, *then* and *because* can be explored by pupils very easily in a Logo activity:

If I rotate my shape by 10 degrees 36 times I shall get back to where I started because there are 360 degrees in a full turn.

- The roamer in China has been renamed YOU-YOU.
- The word *robot* comes from the Czech word *robota* which means 'forced labour'.

- Whilst simulations of control technology are helpful, they should never replace the real thing.
- Always encourage pupils to predict what will happen before they actually run the program.
- Promote debugging of inaccurate programs as a necessary and worthwhile exercise.

- Create and display help cards when investigating Logo. Pupils may need help to load the program, start a new file, close and save their file, recall a previously saved file, and print work.
- Help younger pupils program the Roamer by creating cardboard versions of each key on the Roamer's key pad. They can then sequence these with greater speed, predict what will happen before actually entering the commands

on the key pad, and also copy the command line at the end
if the need arises. If the instructions do not produce the
desired result, pupils will also still have their original
instructions visually in front of them, which they can very
easily edit.

● Always have a supply of spare batteries for the Roamer,
as flat batteries in the middle of a session are extremely
frustrating.

● Create your own Roamer mats. Number lines can be
created on the reverse side of wallpaper. Larger mats that
may incorporate topic work can be created by sticking 4 or
5 lengths of wallpaper together.

● Before starting a control project, check that all sensors
and switches are working properly.

Logo robots

Younger children can be introduced to simple programming
activities by playing 'robots'. Choose one person to be the
'robot' (this can be the teacher or an older pupil if the class
are not ready) and then explain to the whole class that this
robot only understands a special language called Logo.
Briefly explain fd, bk, rt 90 and lt 90 commands. Tell the
children that if they are not completely accurate, the robot
will not understand. Fd 1 will instruct the robot to take 1
step forward.

Blindfold the robot, then hold up a piece of paper which
tells the class where to send the robot. Ask for volunteers to
instruct the robot. Pupils should quickly realize that they
need to be precise and phrases such as 'Move back a bit' are
not sufficient.

Debugging

To stress the importance and acknowledge the real need to
develop debugging skills, pupils should be given a set of
programs to test and then, if necessary, debug. Before
testing, ask pupils to predict the outcome of running the
program.

For example, in the following example:

Program to draw a rectangle:
Repeat 2 [fd 50 rt 90 fd 50 rt 90]

pupils should instantly pick up that a rectangle would be an
impossibility as the two sides indicated in the square
brackets are equal.

Useful websites

www.members.home.net/tgla/ – Lots of Logo information.
www.geocities.com/collegepark/lab/2276 – Inspire pupils
by visiting a Logo art gallery!

Software

The Crystal Rainforest 2000 – an interactive adventure that
introduces and develops Logo skills; *Mission Control* –
introduces control technology without the need for actual
equipment. Both are available from Sherston Software (tel:
01666 843200, www.sherston.com).
Thomas the Clown – designed for pre-readers, this piece of
software begins to develop young children's logical and
sequencing skills. Available from Longman Logotron (tel:
01223 425558).
The adventures of Hilary – a set of thematic control projects
which comes with all the necessary construction materials
for each model. Comes with a guide and full instructions.
Can be used with the Sensci Control box (see below).

Hardware

SenSci Control Box – a control box that has four inputs and
four outputs together with the necessary software required.
A very affordable option, suitable for Windows 95 and
above. Available from Valiant Technology Ltd (tel: 020 8673
2233, www.valiant-technology.com).
Discovery Primary Pack – includes hardware, software,
pupils' and teachers' books. Designed to provide a one-stop
solution to control, monitoring and sensing. Available from
Economatics (tel: 0114 281 3344, www.economatics.co.uk).

Books

Mathematics through WinLogo (Longman Logotron).
Control through Logo (Scholastic).

Chapter 4
The Information Superhighway

C omputers have been around (even in schools) for more than a decade, but the greatest revolution in their use has taken place only in the last few years. Put simply, this revolution has been brought about by the ever-increasing use of computers to communicate. Electronic mail (e-mail) and the Internet now let us communicate with others and access information from anywhere in the world at the cost of a local telephone call. Where the school's resources were once contained within the boundary of its walls, they now reach far beyond, to every museum, art gallery and educational institution you could want to visit.

This chapter looks at the Internet, the World Wide Web and e-mail, and how you can make use of them in your teaching – including how you can set up your own website.

The Internet

Subject facts

What is it?

The Internet is a worldwide network of computers, linked together to form a global system of communication. The Internet is neither owned nor governed by any single person, authority or organization. It has revolutionized communications, is about to storm commerce, and is well on the way to transforming education.

History

The Internet has its origins in the US military. Fears of a breakdown in communications after a nuclear attack were the driving force behind research to establish a decentralized system of communication which could continue to operate despite the destruction of some of its links. The new Packet Switching Technology (PST) provided a network that could survive even if parts of it were destroyed. Packet switching involves data being broken into smaller units (packets) that are routed through a network to its destination where the separate packets are put back together. If any parts of the network were destroyed, packets could be redirected along an alternative path.

The first version of the Internet was trialled in 1969. This network was designed for academics, though in a very short space of time the network has expanded exponentially. Now there are more than 200 million users worldwide and thousands of new websites added every day.

Getting online

Provided you have the necessary hardware and software anybody can access the Internet. You will need:
● a modem, ideally with a speed of 33.6Kbps or better.
● communication software (this will be supplied with the modem or by your Internet service provider)
● a subscription to an Internet Service Provider (this could be your LEA, a free service or a commercial provider)
● a telephone line.

Costs

Computers are connected to the Internet via telephone lines. Charges for use are therefore generated each time a computer goes online. There are many different pricing policies that are available, but competition is fierce and as a result the consumer has benefited. It is important to find a pricing policy that suits your needs. For instance, if Internet access will mainly take place during daytime hours, a flat-rate telephone charge will be better than a tiered one, where there are peak and off-peak rates.

ISDN

For schools the most common form of connection to the Internet is going to be an ISDN (Integrated Services Digital Network) line. This uses standard telephone lines and specialist modems to offer a higher speed of data transfer. ISDN2 enables two voice conversations and up to 100 data transmissions to be carried out simultaneously.

Cable

Most parts of the UK now have access to cable television and cable companies can also offer Internet access using the same high-speed cables. Although it requires special modems, cable technology can support more demanding uses (video conferencing, for example) more easily than standard telephone lines.

Leased lines

If continuous access is needed, a leased line is a possible option. A leased line is rented and charges are set in advance. Charges are not related to time spent on the Internet as access is constant. This is a fairly expensive option and only suitable for larger institutions.

Modem matters

Whilst most people know they need a modem to get online, few will know exactly what it does. Apart from linking the computer to another computer on the Internet via a telephone line, a modem acts as a translator. Computers are digital machines that deal in binary code while telephone lines deal in analogue signals. A modem therefore converts the computer's digital data into analogue signals ready to travel down telephone lines, and will also turn returning analogue signals back into digital signals for the computer.

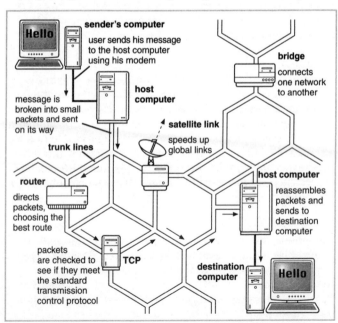

A journey across Cyberspace

The concept of sending data, which may take the form of text, pictures or audio files, around the world in very short spaces of time is the Internet's biggest allure. While there are physical parts that make up the Internet (computers, modems, telephone lines), the whole concept is very ethereal, and as such difficult to visualize.

Newsgroups

Newsgroups are basically discussion forums for like-minded people. They are able to share views, facts and opinions by posting messages on electronic notice boards for all members to read. Membership to a newsgroup is normally through subscription and special software is required to access your newsgroup.

There are literally thousands of newsgroups available, which are broadly divided by following main categories:

Comp. Computer topics	*News. News related topics*
Rec. Recreational, sport	*Sci. Science*
Soc. Society	*Talk. Discussion groups*
Alt. Alternative groups	*Misc. Miscellaneous*

These divisions are known as hierarchies and each group can be further sub-divided, each time becoming more and more specific.

IRC (Internet Relay Chat)

Unlike newsgroups where discussions are carried out over time, IRC is based around real-time discussion. Participants communicate through text messages, often with many other people at once. Just as newsgroups have different subject groupings, IRC has many different 'channels' where people with varying interests gather. Care must be taken with the use of IRC in schools as most chat is unregulated. It has also built up a reputation for being a popular haunt for the mischievous. Accepting unrequested files must therefore be avoided and pupils' use of IRC must always be closely monitored.

Management issues

There are many questions which need to be answered when setting up an Internet connection for school. The following are just a few to consider.

Where will the connected computer be based?

If you are connecting a single computer to the Internet this needs great thought, especially as changing location may prove expensive. Should the computer be based in a classroom (where one teacher may be expected to take an extended role in supervision and instruction) or should it be in a more neutral position such as the school office or library, where access is a little more open? Would the latter have implications for security and supervision? If you have a networked system in which all computers have Internet access, would it be better to have them in a cluster so that a whole class can access the Internet at the same time, or to have one connected computer in every classroom?

Who should have access?
If your resources are limited, it may be better to target specific year groups for termly units of Internet access – this would of course have implications for curriculum planning.

Apart from pupils, it is also vital that teachers have time to access the Internet, not just for lesson preparation but for personal career development too. Training may be an issue and after-school taster sessions for teachers may be a good start.

How should Internet access be supervised?
All computer use by children should be supervised, particularly if they are able to gain unrestricted access to the Internet. You should consider purchasing filtering software if your service provider does not offer a filtered service (as many educational providers do). This will deny access to unsuitable sites or files with certain keywords. A number of packages exist, including *Net Nanny* and *Cyber Patrol*, and most will allow different levels of access for teachers and pupils. It's important, too, to teach children how to use the Internet responsibly.

How can the Internet be used to enhance the learning process?
Anyone who has used the Internet will know just how easy it is to surf fairly aimlessly, and how easy it is to be distracted by dancing hamsters. While there are certain circumstances where this luxury may be acceptable, it would not be justified in an educational context.

Lessons based around the Internet need to have clearly planned learning objectives which are achievable, appropriate and structured. In this way, and set within a meaningful educational context, the Internet can become a powerful learning tool for pupils. Some suggestions are included in the Teaching Ideas section on page 141.

Are there opportunities for parental involvement?
Parental involvement in schools has long been seen as
being extremely beneficial. Parents by no means need to be
Internet experts; their roles should be seen as facilitators.
There will be times when a search can call up articles that
can be very challenging, and in these circumstances parents
can be of great assistance.

Who will have access to e-mail?
Should all pupils have their own e-mail address? Should
e-mail dialogue be carried out on a class/group basis? Even
if you do not plan to give all pupils an e-mail address at this
stage, it's advisable to choose a system which can offer this.

Are there training needs?
Many of the above issues, together with the practicalities of
the Internet, need to be addressed in training sessions.
Training should be curriculum-led to make the best use of
the Internet in an educational context. Teachers also need
time to develop their own confidence in using the
technology and integrating it with the rest of the
curriculum.

Acceptable use
Many schools find it helpful to create an Acceptable Use
Policy for Internet use. This can cover privacy of passwords,
not using abusive or offensive language, not reading other
people's mail or deleting other people's files, amongst other
issues. An agreement that pupils and parents endorse, such
as one that clearly accepts the school's Acceptable Use
Policy, signed by pupils and giving parental permission for
pupils to use the Internet, may be useful.

Netiquette
In the absence of formal regulation, those who use the
Internet are well known for regulating themselves, and a
system of rules regarding acceptable behaviour has
emerged, known as netiquette. Netiquette, for example,
dictates that when communicating through text it is
considered rude to type in all capitals This is hard to read,
and is the written equivalent of shouting. Spamming, which
is needlessly sending the same unsolicited message to many
recipients is also frowned upon. Apart from these rules,
pupils should be taught from the outset that a common-
sense approach should be taken. Bad language and
argumentative discourse for the sake of 'a bit of a laugh' are
far too easy given the degree of anonymity a pupil can have.

Pupils should also be encouraged to act responsibly if they do come in to contact with inappropriate material and behaviour. They should know who to report such matters to, and a strategy to deal with such incidences should be in place in school with the relevant staff aware of the procedures which need to be followed. The Internet Watch Foundation is an organization that schools can contact to report illegal material on the Internet. They can be contacted on 0845 600 8844. Schools should also contact their LEA which should have a monitoring procedure in place. Teachers need to remember, however, that not all offensive material is illegal.

Why you need to know these facts

The Internet has proved to be a huge phenomenon, affecting people in all walks of life. It has simultaneously influenced industry, commerce, government, leisure and education. As educators we must therefore ensure that pupils are given the necessary skills to take advantage of such a resource, not only for its educational potential but for the practicalities of our pupils' future lives. Teachers need to get to grips with new technologies and find ways of successfully integrating their use in the classroom so that learning is enhanced. The practicalities involved in the initial setting-up stages are considerable and many decisions will often need to be made at management level. Once in place, however, it is up to teachers to harness the educational potential of the Internet, extract all that is good, dismiss all that is irrelevant, and protect pupils from all that is offensive.

Amazing facts

● The term 'cyberspace', often used when talking about all things related to the Internet, was first used by William Gibson in his novel *Neuromancer*, published in 1984.
● Users of the Internet are often called netizens.
● The James Bond film *The World is not Enough* was stolen and made available on the Internet for free before its official release.

Golden rules

● Never allow pupils to exchange personal details such as addresses and telephone numbers with other people over the Internet.
● Tell children that they should always report to an adult any material or suggestions they come across which they feel uncomfortable with.

How can I open a PDF file that I have downloaded?
Many documents on the Internet are transmitted as a PDF
file (Portable Document Format). To open them on your
computer you will need *Adobe Acrobat Reader*. Download
this for free from Adobe's website at www.adobe.com.

*What is the difference between the Internet and the
World Wide Web?*
The Internet is the actual infrastructure of the global
network of computers that provides the means for data to
travel from computer to computer, while the World Wide
Web is a user-friendly way of accessing files stored on
computers that are connected to the Internet.

What are fibre-optic cables?
Fibre-optic cables differ from traditional copper twisted
cables in that they are made from thin strands of glass.
These new cables are capable of sending more data down
phone lines at greater speeds and with increased efficiency,
and may one day replace existing phone and cable TV
networks.

The whole concept of the Internet is a difficult one to grasp
because of its sheer magnitude and intangible nature. The
Journey into Cyberspace diagram on page 136 may be a
useful representation for the pupils to recreate. Obviously
the different elements of the diagram need to be discussed
beforehand, giving pupils a greater understanding.

A more individual approach would be to allow pupils to
come up with their own graphical representations of the
Internet. Examples of how the concept has been tackled by
other people (in posters, books and magazines) would prove
a useful starting point.

In small groups give pupils the names of different
occupations and ask them to discuss reasons why the
Internet would be useful to them.

Useful websites
National Grid for Learning – www.ngfl.gov.uk; contains
many resources and useful links. The Virtual Teacher
Centre is an absolute must.
www.child.net – promotes child-safe Internet use, with lots
of advice and help for parents and teachers.
QCA – www.qca.org.uk.

Microsoft – www.microsoft.com has a wealth of information and many freebies to download too.
www.online-teachers.net – internet access especially designed for teachers; includes many useful resources
National Curriculum site – www.nc.uk.net.
BECTA – www.becta.org.uk.
National Association for Co-ordinators and Teachers of IT – www.acitt.org.uk.
National Association of Advisors for Computers in Education – www.naace.org.uk.
Birmingham Grid for Learning – www.bgfl.org; one of a number of local grids for learning and an excellent resource for teachers, parents and pupils.

Software
Internet Microworld: Statistics for Education – this allows you to explore the Internet before going online. Available from Statistics for Education (tel: 01279 652183).

Books
Introducing the Internet: A beginner's Guide to the Internet – Primary Education;
Internet Activities – The Chalkface Project (CyberSurfer Owl)
The Internet for Beginners (Usborne Computer Guides).
From Chalkboard to Internet: the Internet Starter's Handbook, (BECTA).

Vocabulary

Host computer – a host computer links a user's computer to the Internet.
Internet Service Providers – companies that provide access to the Internet via powerful host computers. Otherwise known as ISPs.
Baud Rate – speed at which a modem can send information down a telephone line.
e-commerce – buying goods and services online.
Moderated newsgroup – a newsgroup where all postings are checked by moderators before being published.
Server – a powerful computer that stores, sorts and distributes data on the Internet.
Client – a computer that accesses data from a server.
Leased line – a permanent telephone line connection to the Internet.
Online – connected to the Internet.
Offline – not connected to the Internet.
Modem – MOdulator/DEModulator: a device to connect computers via telephone lines.

Acronyms
ARPA – Advanced Research Projects Agency.
TCP – Transmission Control Protocol. A standard of communication that has been established so that all computers on the Internet 'speak' the same language.
ISDN – Integrated Services Digital Network. An extremely fast digital phone line.
URL – Uniform Resource Locator. The address which identifies a website.
WWW – World Wide Web. A collection of interactive pages found on the Internet.
Kbps – Kilobits per second. The speed of data transmission is measured in Kbps (or Mbps – Megabits per second).
FTP – File Transfer Protocol. A system which allows you to transfer files from a computer on the Internet to your own.
BBS – Bulletin Board System.
DNS – Domain Name System.
PDF – Portable Document Format.

The World Wide Web

What is it?

Subject facts

The World Wide Web has been the main reason for the recent explosion in the use of the Internet. The Web is the most popular part of the Internet and consists of millions of interactive, hypertext documents. Access to these is simple and the wealth of information they provide is awesome.

What is a URL?
Each web page on the Web has its own unique Uniform Resource Locator (or URL). Whilst this may look complicated, it is in fact very straightforward, and can tell you quite a lot about the origin of the document. Take a closer look at the following example:

http://www.scholastic.co.uk/education/homepage.html

http:// stands for hypertext transmission protocol, and indicates to the computer the type of data it is about to receive.
www. tells you that the site is on the World Wide Web.
scholastic.co.uk is known as the domain name and indicates the type of organization the host computer belongs to. In this case, **Scholastic** is the name of the organization, the **.co** means that it is a commercial company, and the **.uk**

indicates that it is UK based. **/education/homepage.html** is
the filepath and indicates where to look for a specific file on
the host computer. In this case the document is called
homepage.html (*.html* indicating that it is written in
hypertext markup language, specifically designed for the
Web) in a folder named *education*.

The URL can give you a very good indication as to the
type of organization the website belongs to. The following
lists the most common.

Domain name	What type of organization?
.edu	Educational institution in America.
.ac	Used for all other academic institutions. Always followed by a country code: .ac.uk.
.sch	Relatively new type of domain name, reserved for UK primary and secondary schools. Followed by a country code, such as .sch.uk.
.org	Non-commercial organizations and charities, often followed by a country code: .org.uk.
.com	Commercial organization – originally used exclusively by American companies, but now seen worldwide.
.co	Commercial organization – used by non-American companies. Always followed by a country code: .co.uk, or .co.fr in France.
.gov	Government department – often followed by a country code, except in the USA
.net	A variant of .com and .co.uk, often used for exclusively Internet-based companies or organizations.

Browsing

The activity of viewing web pages is referred to as browsing
or surfing (the two terms are interchangeable). Before you
can do this you will need a Web browser – a piece of
software specially designed to do just this. Web pages are
written in HTML (Hypertext Markup Language), and a
browser enables your computer to interpret this and
convert it into a format that you can view. The two most
common browsers are *Netscape Navigator* and *Microsoft
Internet Explorer,* and most new computers come with one
or the other already installed. Failing that, modem software
often includes a browser, or you can download the latest
version from the Internet.

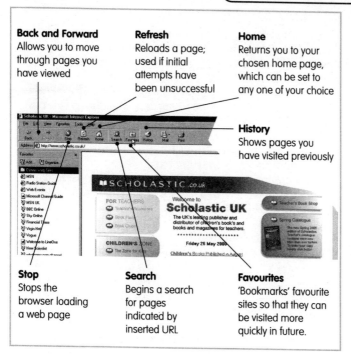

Back and Forward
Allows you to move through pages you have viewed

Refresh
Reloads a page; used if initial attempts have been unsuccessful

Home
Returns you to your chosen home page, which can be set to any one of your choice

History
Shows pages you have visited previously

Stop
Stops the browser loading a web page

Search
Begins a search for pages indicated by inserted URL

Favourites
'Bookmarks' favourite sites so that they can be visited more quickly in future.

A good Web browser should allow you to:
- view web pages
- bookmark favourite sites
- download material
- save and print files
- navigate web pages with ease.

What is a web page?

A web page is a document that is accessible on the Web. It normally contains hypertext, otherwise known as links that connect to other pages with the click of a mouse button (underlined text on a web page is normally a link to other material on the same, or a different, site). This means that a web page is very different in nature from any other type of document. It is in fact a non-linear document with a radically new approach to text organization. In turn the reader is expected to take an active role, making decisions about where to go next, what to read and what not to read along the way. The page can be made up of a combination of text, sound, video, animation and graphical images. There is often an opportunity for the reader to give immediate feedback via e-mail. The whole experience for the reader is very empowering.

Searching

The Web's greatest virtue – its vast and ever-increasing size – is, unfortunately, also its greatest problem. How do you find the information you are looking for? Locating a particular web page that you have a complete URL for is easy. You simply type the URL in to your Web browser, press ENTER and wait for the page to appear. Note, however, that you must be accurate when you key in any URL – they are usually lower case and have no spaces between letters. If you mis-type any part of the URL, the browser will simply tell you that the page does not exist.

If you don't know the URL for the page you are looking for, you will need to use a search engine which will find as much information as possible on any given topic.

What is a search engine?

A search engine aims to index the contents of the Internet, either manually, using editors, or using specially designed software. Most search engines have a facility for people to register their web pages, so that searching for particular keywords will locate them.

Search engines are divided into two types: those that search by keywords (such as Alta Vista) or those that are hierarchical, such as Yahoo! The latter groups sites into subject areas and the user gradually narrows down his or her search. So, if you wanted to find out what whales eat, your search path in Yahoo! would look something like this:

Animals > Mammals > Whales > Feeding

Keyword searches

A keyword is a phrase or word which sums up the contents of a web page. When a search engine is instructed by you to look for a keyword, it will scan its index and find all those pages which contain your keyword.

Care needs to be taken when using keywords and practice will improve technique. It's worth reading the search engine's help files and learning the syntax used. Note that when faced with more than one word, a search engine will normally look for either word, thus extending your hotlist. Narrowing down a search is the key.

Search tips

Plus and minus signs

To broaden or narrow down a search, plus and minus signs can be used very effectively. For example, if you wanted to find out about mammals except for humans you would type:

> *mammals – humans* or *mammals NOT humans.*

If you wanted to find out about classical music you would type

> *classical + music* or *classical AND music.*

Narrow your search

Don't search the whole Internet if you know what you are looking for is UK based. Most search engines will allow you to confine your search to UK websites.

Multiple meanings

Remember that some words have multiple meanings, so add synonyms to help clarify meaning. For example, if your class was doing a topic on drug abuse, searching for *drugs* would find, amongst other things, the world's drug companies, thousands of medicines and hundreds of American drug stores. Searching for *narcotics* would be more effective, since this is the preferred term in the USA.

Huge hotlists

Many searches will result in hundreds of possible matches ('hits'), if not more, although it's normally not worth going beyond the first ten. Search engines will usually decide on an order with the best matches at the top of the list.

Use phrases

Some search engines will have the option to look for phrases, where the order of words is kept. This can often be done by enclosing words in quotation marks. *'The golden temple'* will look for a web page that has this exact phrase, for example. This will probably make the search far more productive and cut out all the pages which may refer only to temples or all things golden!

Wild cards

By using a wild card (denoted by an asterisk *) a keyword is made more adaptable. By placing the asterisk after the keyword, the search engine will look for different word endings. For example, *teach** will find pages with the words *teach, teaching, teaches* and *teacher*. Instantly the search has encompassed a greater degree of detail and should now pick up a greater number of relevant pages.

Advanced searches

Some search engines allow even greater control of the

search. Advanced searches usually allow the user to: state which part of the web to search, search according to when pages were published, select how much detail is provided about each hit, or rank the order of keywords used.

Points to remember
● No search engine gives complete coverage of the Web.
● Owing to the fluidity of the Internet and the speed of changes, you can expect a few missing URLs where search engines have not been able to keep up with changes.
● Most search engines are not case-sensitive – it does not matter whether a word is typed in capitals or lower case.

Child-friendly search engines
An offshoot of Yahoo!, Yahoo!ligans (www.yahooligans.com) is a search engine specifically designed for children and contains excellent guides for teachers and parents. It also evaluates sites against its '4 As' before adding them to its listings: Accessibility, Accuracy, Appropriateness and Appeal. Searchopolis (www.searchopolis.com) is a great starting point with items like word of the day, today's birthdays, and today in history.

Filtering
Filtering is the process by which inappropriate sites on the Web are blocked so that pupils cannot gain access to them. This is usually done using software that blocks sites containing keywords, the obvious examples in education being *sex* and *violence* (although it is worth noting that some websites contain highly offensive racial material which would also be unsuitable). A list of inappropriate URLs is created and then access to these blocked.
There are many solutions on the market and whether you approach filtering on a school by school basis or an LEA basis, the reality of the situation is that there will always be inconsistencies, with appropriate sites being blocked and quite inappropriate sites slipping through the net. The process will always rely on a proactive approach that will aim to address and put right the inconsistencies.

Safe havens
With the vastness of the Internet comes a degree of unpredictability. New websites are being published on a daily basis and monitoring them becomes an almost impossible task. The response to such problems has been the implementation of intranets which offer a safe, monitored environment while providing many facets of the

Internet. If the Internet is akin to a vast wilderness without boundaries and where anything goes, an intranet is like a closed community with set boundaries which is policed closely. Many commercial solutions based on this 'safe haven' principle are on offer, and these provide schools with attractive features.

An intranet is a cut-down version of the Internet which uses browsers to view the pages, but access is restricted to only the pages on the intranet. This system is particularly useful for downloading websites (or parts of them) that are popular so that searching time is not wasted and they can be viewed offline. Once an intranet has been set up, it can also contain materials written by teachers themselves.

Educational services

To help teachers and pupils get the most from the Internet, many products have been developed. *AngliaCampus* and RM's *Eduweb* are two such products. Both provide pupil-friendly interfaces with easy search facilities that guide pupils to relevant, educationally sound sites.

A note on copyright

It is vital that teachers and pupils are aware that materials published on the Web are covered by the same copyright laws as other non-electronic publications. However, much is available on the Internet which can be freely downloaded. For example, public domain images that do not belong to anybody may be downloaded and used without any consent whatsoever. Websites should state clearly whether material on the site is copyright or not. If it is, then permission may be sought from the Webmaster (an e-mail link usually allows you to do this).

Integrating the Internet with the curriculum

The Internet truly knows no boundaries. There is a Web page (or indeed a whole site) for virtually every area of the curriculum and more. However, for effective use of a relevant Web page some guidelines need to drawn.

● In the early days of exploring the Web, it's a good idea to plan searches on paper and to talk about suitable keywords before you start.

● Give pupils specific objectives when searching the Web. The important thing is not just to find a useful website, but to use the information it contains. If pupils are searching for information on amphibians, for example, ask each group to find out all they can on a particular amphibian and then (copyright permitting) incorporate the information in their own presentation to the rest of the class. With older children, encourage them to rewrite the information they have found in their own words.

● Encourage pupils to be critical of everything they find. Who has written it? Are their views biased? How can we tell if the information is accurate?

● Ask pupils to make an evaluation of the sites they visit using pre-determined criteria, which may help future visitors to the site. For example, how useful was the information? How easy was it to find? How easy was it to read and understand? Was it easy to navigate the site?

Why you need to know these facts

The World Wide Web is where most of the Internet's treasures lie. To be able to use it efficiently and effectively is vital. As the National Grid for Learning and other community grids develop, a centralized directory of ideas and resources will become available for teachers.

Golden rules

● Never allow pupils to use the Internet without supervision or some system of filtering.
● Always set time limits.
● Never allow pupils to download files without some sort of virus protection in place.

Amazing facts

● Yahoo!, one of the leading search engines on the Internet, started off as a small project housed in a trailer at Stanford University. It was called 'Jerry's guide to the World Wide Web' after its co-founder Jerry Yang.
● The longest registered domain name was named after a famous Welsh village. It is... www.llanfairpwllgwyngyllgo-gerychwyrndrobwllllantysiliogogogoch.co.uk
● The search engine Alta Vista had to buy its domain name from a company that had already registered it. It is reported that the purchase price was well over $3million!

Common misconceptions

Everything you find on the Internet is accurate.
Sadly this is far from the case. Because there is no regulation of websites, anyone can publish material, however inaccurate (or deliberately misleading) it may be. Pupils need to be taught to be critical of any information they find and look for bias as well as inaccuracies.

- If you want to cut down on the time it takes to download sites, set your browser so that it doesn't download images. There will usually be an option to do this.
- You can stop downloading a page at any time by clicking on the *Stop* button found in your browser.
- If you have a favourite site that you wish to visit on a regular basis, use a bookmark so that you do not have to enter the URL each time. Bookmarks are similar to Windows' shortcuts.
- If you want to view pages offline, save them onto your hard drive using the *Save As* option in the *File* menu.
- If you want to save a graphic you have found on a web page, place your mouse pointer onto to the picture and click once with your right mouse button. A *Save As* dialogue box should appear. Choose a location for it on your hard disk.
- As most of the resources on the Internet are based in the USA, the best time to go online is when the Americans are asleep! You will find it faster to connect in the mornings for this reason.

Why does it sometimes take so long to connect to a website?
The Internet may be very busy or the site you are trying to connect to may only support a certain number of connections.

Is there a risk of viruses when downloading files?
Viruses are always something to worry about whenever you download a file. Downloading a file from a reputable commercial site should not pose too much of a threat. Anti-virus software is available that will check your downloads for such hazards.

When I try to look at a website I get a 'time-out'. Why?
Your browser will usually try to connect for a set time, and if a connection is not made, it will stop. One of the most common reasons for a connection failure is that the site has moved or the Internet is just too busy, meaning that the superhighway is in a bit of a jam.

What's the difference between a search engine and a browser?
Strictly speaking, a search engine's primary focus is to index and locate websites using keywords or hierarchical searches. A Web browser, on the other hand, is the software

needed to view web pages. However, things are changing. To compete in the ferociously competitive arena of the Internet, search engines and browsers are all beginning to offer similar, integrated software that provides a 'total' solution to surfing the Web.

What is a 'zipped' file?

A 'zipped' file is one that has been compressed. Large files are normally zipped to decrease the amount of space they take up. While this results in shorter download times it also means you cannot view them until you have 'unzipped' them. For this you will need some special software. Most popular is *Winzip* for Windows, which may be downloaded as shareware from the Internet from www.winzip.com.

Teaching ideas

Searching for answers

● Develop pupils' search techniques by giving groups of children the task of drawing up keyword lists for different subjects. How successful were their searches? What did they learn? Which words need to be avoided?
● As a class project pupils could be asked to review specific websites. Depending on age and ability, the constructing of the review questionnaire could be the first task set. A database of reviewed websites could be built up over time.
● Explore the hierarchical structure of search engines like Yahoo!ligans. Give pupils a specific question – for example, 'how do frogs breathe?' Ask pupils to construct on paper possible search paths. How successful were these for the real search?
● Direct pupils to specific websites linked to a planned curriculum topic. Ask pupils to answer a set of questions based on the site. (Clearly this task demands a thorough knowledge of the site by the teacher. Links should be explored and pupils' ability to navigate the site as well as assimilate information should be tested.)

Vocabulary

Surfing – used to describe exploration of the Internet.
Web browser – software required to surf the Internet.
Webmaster – the person in charge of a website.
Homepage – the first page of a website, rather like a welcome page.
Upload – to copy files from your own computer to another computer on the Internet.
Download – to copy files from another computer on the Internet to your own computer.

Java – an advanced programming language used to incorporate animations within web pages.

Hotlist – a summative list of hits constructed by a search engine in response to a specific search.

Search engine – a program that searches the World Wide Web for pages of information on a specific topic.

Hypertext links – words or pictures that are highlighted or underlined to show that they link to other pages or sites; when you point to a hypertext link with your mouse, the pointer will change to a pointing finger symbol. Also known as hyperlinks.

Software

Resources

Bess – an Internet filtering service specifically aimed at parents and schools. More information is available from www.bess.net

Books

World Wide Web for Beginners (Usborne Computer Guides).

Useful websites

www.cln.org – although a Canadian site, there is much that teachers can gain from this resource. It provides advice, information and resources on topics ranging from computer viruses to science lessons. There is also the opportunity to sign up for the free weekly newsletter that comes packed with many new sites to visit.

www.etour.com – a slightly different way to search the Web. It sells itself by boasting that users do not have to search the Web at all. Instead, just fill out a questionnaire that will highlight your interests and let the e-tour find sites that match these. It's surprisingly good and avoids typing endless lists of URLs.

www.mape.org.uk – Micros and Primary Education site.

www.surfmonkey.com – a good site to recommend to parents. Download the surfmonkey browser and many useful child-safe features are offered. Monitored chat rooms and e-mail, and plenty of sites that are especially suitable for children. Great for school use too.

www.bbc.co.uk/education/webwise – designed to introduce adults and children alike to the Internet. Well written in clear language.

www.educate.org.uk – an invaluable site for the primary teacher. Updated on a monthly basis, the site provides worksheets, articles and reviews, together with an index of subject-specific websites.

www.homeworkelephant.free-online.co.uk – an excellent site to recommend to parents and pupils alike. Designed to help pupils with all their homework needs. Lots of things of interest to teachers too.

www.vtc.ngfl.gov.uk – the Virtual Teacher Centre on the National Grid for Learning has plenty of links to useful sites for all subjects in the primary curriculum.

Building your own website

Subject facts

Many schools are now setting up their own websites. Having a Web presence will allow a school to:
● promote itself
● share ideas and resources
● build up links with other schools.
By setting up a website, you can achieve this not only on a national scale but on a global one.

What you need
It can be quite a major undertaking to set up a website, and you will need:
● a member of staff to co-ordinate the project and keep it up to date
● space on the Internet for you to publish your web pages – many ISPs now offer this service free of charge
● a method of creation
● a scanner to digitize pictures or photographs to include
● a lot of enthusiasm!
You may decide to buy a website design and creation service from a professional design company. This will not require any technical knowledge, and you will only be responsible for the content. You will need to bear in mind the costs for updating the site in addition to the initial design, however. Alternatively, you may create your own site using an editor program. This will turn your word-processed document into a web page by automatically inserting the necessary HTML code. If you are a confident ICT user, you may be brave enough to create a website from scratch using a simple word processor and 'raw' HTML code.

Once you have decided to create a website, the next step is to start the planning process for it.

There are many things to consider when approaching this task but the first port of call is easy. Visit other school's websites which have already been published. Take a close look at content, organization and design, and let pupils make their own evaluations. A prepared questionnaire allowing pupils to comment on things they liked, disliked and would change will form a strong foundation for your own school website.

Common features of a school website

At the very start you will need a homepage. Rather like the front cover of a book, this needs to be appealing and capture the attention of the audience so that they will want to explore further. It needs to give some indication as to the content of the site and have a clear and easy method of navigation. You could include, for example, the name of the school, the location, a photograph and general description of the school, and links at the top of the page that can direct visitors to different locations with ease. Just as important is a button at the bottom of subsequent pages that will get the visitor back to the homepage.

A web page can become much more fun if the visitor can participate. For example, include a questionnaire for visitors to fill in and then send back to the school, e-mail opportunities, puzzles and simple games to play. Note, however, that creating these extra features is complicated, and requires more technical knowledge. For forms and other interactive features, knowledge of CGI (Common Gateway Interface) is required. Help is at hand at www.freedback.com; this site does all the hard work and allows you to download many useful items such as forms for inclusion in your own website.

You don't always have to create something yourself to offer. You could include a hyperlink to an FTP site that has something fun or interesting to download. It's a great motivator for pupils to see their works of art on show and a picture gallery to show them off would be ideal. You don't have to stop at pictures – pupils' best work could be showcased at another location. This would of course need updating regularly.

To make a site more interesting, add small sound and video files. A welcome from the headteacher on the homepage is a favourite, but don't stop there, be creative!

Using graphics in web pages

There are basically two types of graphic used in web pages: GIF and JPEG images.

Developed by Compuserve, GIF (Graphics Interchange Format) images are made up of 256 colours. Saving graphics as a GIF will produce larger file sizes but produce better quality images than JPEG images, which are smaller in size but lose more quality and, because they are made up of 16 million colours, need to be viewed on an appropriate monitor.

Of course the easiest way to reduce the file size of an image is to reduce its dimensions. Reducing the size of an image by 25 per cent actually cuts the file size by half, thus halving the time it takes to upload the image too.

Creation the HTML way

HTML is a text-based computer coding language. By using HTML you can create a document that can be viewed on the Web. The following section deals with creating a web page using a simple word processor like *WordPad* (but any other would do), and introduces some basic HTML tags.

HTML code turns an ordinary text document into a web page. HTML tells your Web browser two very important things: that the document is a web page, and how to display text in the document by adding images, links, colour, style and formatting to the plain text of the code in the HTML.

HTML tags

Individual HTML codes are referred to as 'tags'. Tags usually, though not always, come in pairs – one to start the tag and one to end it. The first tag should be placed before the text the effect needs to be applied to and the second should be placed after it.

For example, If you wish the word *fantastic* to appear in bold text then the tags should be placed as follows:

> *<B>FANTASTIC</B>*

Notice that the tag is put inside angle brackets so that the browser knows what is a tag and what is a part of the web page. Apart from the angle brackets, most closing tags have a forward slash too to indicate the end of the tag.

Sizing text

There are six different font sizes available in HTML. Size one is the smallest, and size six the largest. To have the word *fantastic* appear in size 5, the following tags would need to be applied:

> *<FONT SIZE=5>FANTASTIC</FONT>*

A splash of colour

Unless you add appropriate tags, a browser will display text in black, normally on a white background. To change the colour of your text and the background is easy to do, and can create more impact. You could create your school's website in school colours, for example.

Together with the correct tags a colour code is needed This may be a hexadecimal colour code (such as those below) for precise colours, or the name of a colour for common colours. The following table lists a few to start you off:

Hexadecimal Code	Colour
#CD6090	Pink
#CD8500	Orange
#FF0000 or 'red'	Red
#FFFF00 or 'yellow'	Yellow
#FFFFFF or 'white'	White
#000000 or 'black'	Black
#00FF00 or 'green'	Green
#0000FF or 'blue'	Blue
#888888 or 'grey'	Grey
#8B5A2B	Brown

For example, to change the colour of text to blue, enter the following code:

```
<FONT COLOR="blue">fantastic</FONT>
```

If you wanted each letter of the word in a different colour then the tags should be applied before and after each letter using the desired colour codes (but remember that the text should remain readable!).

To change the colour of text on a whole page, a code needs to be inserted to the <BODY> tag, which sets the style for the whole document. For example:

```
<BODY TEXT="red">
</BODY> (closing tag is unchanged)
```

The above tags would result in all text being displayed in red.

Breaking up blocks of text

A web page with a lot of text can be a turn-off for any reader. Simple items to break down the wall of words are effective and easy to achieve. The following table lists some.

Desired Effect	HTML Code
To start a new paragraph	Type <P> in front of the first word of the new paragraph and </P> at the end of the paragraph.
To start a new line	A single tag is required. Type where you wish the new line to start.
Headings	HTML has six different sizes of headings. <H1> is the largest and <H6> is the smallest. To display the word *fantastic* as a level 1 heading type <H1>FANTASTIC</H1>
Lines	Horizontal lines can be used to divide up a web page. To draw a line add the code <HR> where you wish the line to be. This will draw a line across the width of the page. By adding additional information to the tag you can change the appearance of the lines. Lines can be aligned to the left or right, be made thicker or thinner, and can be any width. It is important to note, however, that lines are automatically centred unless otherwise instructed. So <HR WIDTH="50%"> will draw a line half the width of the page and will be centred. To have it drawn from the left and extend to the centre you would have to type <HR WIDTH="50%" ALIGN="LEFT">
Numbered Lists	To create a numbered list (say a top ten, for example) use the <OL> tag to start and end your ordered list, and begin each item within the list with a <LI> tag. For example, *<OL><LI>Cricket<LI>Football</OL>* will produce: 1. Cricket 2. Football
Bulleted lists	A simple, unordered list can be created in the same way as a numbered list, but by using the <UL> tag to start and end the list. For example, *<UL><LI>Cricket<LI>Football</UL>* will produce: • Cricket • Football
To create an e-mail link, otherwise known as a mailto link	<A HREF="MAILTO:avneet@scholastic.co.uk">Contact me</A>

Inserting pictures

To embed a picture file you will need to place it in the same directory as your source document and type the following where you want your picture to appear:

> *<IMG SRC="picture.jpg">*

Add the name of your picture file, making sure you use the correct file name. To include alternative text that describes your picture for people viewing without pictures, add the following

> *<IMG SRC="picture.jpg" ALT="a picture">*

Pictures can be aligned on your web page to the left, centre or right, just as with text:

> *<CENTER><IMG SRC="picture.jpg"></CENTER>*

will centre your image. Note that the word <CENTER> is the American spelling, as HTML originates from the USA; using English spellings will not work – this also applies to <COLOR> tags.

Creating hyperlinks

Hyperlinks are connections which link pages within your website or to pages on a different site. They can be characterized by pictures, words or phrases. Once created, your browser will display them either in a different colour or underlined to show their status as a hyperlink. Within your website, to turn the words 'homework tasks' into a hyperlink to the homework page, type the following:

> *<A HREF="homework.html">homework tasks</A>*

making sure, of course, that you do have a page on your website called *homework.html*. You can also link to other websites. To turn the word *Scholastic* into a hyperlink to Scholastic's website type the following:

> *<A HREF="http://www.scholastic.co.uk/">Scholastic</A>*

Pictures can also be used to symbolize a link. To turn a picture of a house into a hyperlink to your homepage, type the following:

> *<A HREF="homepage.htm"><IMG SRC="house.gif"></A>*

Golden rules

- Don't include very large graphic images or sound files on your website, as they will take a very long time to download. People are normally put off, and may not bother at all!
- As a courtesy to those people who are viewing web pages without pictures, include alternative text which will appear in place of the picture. This should provide a brief description of the picture.
- Be careful when including links to other sites, as you have no control over their longevity; carry out regular checks to make sure they are still there.
- Update your website regularly: a site can very easily become stale and out of date.
- If you ever move a file that's part of your web page, make sure you update the relevant links within your source code.
- Don't make individual web pages too long. It is far better to divide your information into smaller sections that link together using hyperlinks.
- To make the uploading of your website easier, save your files in a new folder separate from other files.
- Be careful when experimenting with colour, as some colour combinations make it very difficult for the reader to read your text. Pink on a red background is very difficult to read, while blue on a white background is much better.
- If you are offering a download, specify the size so that people are aware of the download times.
- Always save web pages as .html files when creating them in a simple word processor.
- Sadly, we need to be aware that photographs of young children may appeal to an undesirable audience. Ensure that information is kept to a minimum and does not include addresses or telephone numbers of children. If you are including photographs of children, it is advisable to get parental permission first.

Why you need to know these facts

A school website will become as common as a school logo in a very short time. Small schools will reap benefits as much as the larger ones, if not more so. No school need now feel isolated or cut off from the wider world, as membership to a global community (with schools as far away as the other side of the globe) is one of the benefits that the Internet provides. How a school approaches creating a website is of course a personal choice and one which will be influenced by the experience of leading members of staff.

● Hexadecimal colour codes can describe up to 16 million different colours. Even the human eye cannot distinguish between this many colours, so will see an approximation.
● HTML is platform independent: whether a web page has been created on a Mac, PC or any other computer, all will be able to understand it if using the relevant software.

● If you wish to check the source code (actually see the HTML tags) of a web page, click on the *View* menu in your browser and then *Source*.
● Always type your tags in capitals. It will make your source document easier to read.
● Use your browser to see what your web pages look like (and if there are any errors in them) before you actually upload them. Open your browser and select *File* then *Open*.
● Use plenty of line breaks in your source document so that it is easy to read and edit at a later date. Remember none of the line breaks will be displayed on your actual web page.
● Re-use graphic files more than once on your website. Once the file has been downloaded, subsequent uses will not incur any extra download times.

I've seen school websites which incorporate the school name into their URL. How do they do this?
These schools have registered their own domain name. As long as nobody else has the domain name you want, it is possible to register your own. A government initiative means that all schools in England will automatically get their own .sch.uk domain name. Further domain names can be registered for a fee from a number of companies.

Is it a good idea to include an e-mail link on a website?
Once you give people the opportunity to communicate through e-mail there will always be the danger of abusive communiqués. However, for a school website this channel of communication can lead to very positive gains. It may be useful to have a central e-mail address for all correspondence, and as long as e-mails are checked before pupils can access them, there should not be a problem.

Should I scan pictures at the highest resolution possible?
Definitely not! Various factors will affect the file size of a picture. One is the image's dimensions and the other is the resolution. The higher the resolution, the bigger the file

size. As file sizes should be kept as small as possible, it is far better to stick to a lower resolution. It is important to note that monitors cannot display high resolutions, so scanning a picture at a high resolution may be a complete waste of time. A picture scanned for a web page need only have a resolution of 72dpi.

Vocabulary

Local links – hyperlinks within a website.
Remote link – hyperlinks to sites other than your own.
FTP Client – a program needed to upload your files to your host computer.
NIC – Network Information Centre. This controls the use of domain names, making sure that a particular domain name is only used once.

Resources

If your school wishes to get a website quickly and with the least amount of effort, Questions Publishing Co. Ltd (tel: 0121 212 0919) may have the answer with their new product, Schoolweb.

Useful websites

www.webdeveloper.com – provides useful tutorials and essential advice for first-time HTML programmers.
www.davesite.com/webstation/html – an excellent HTML tutorial that lets your test your newly acquired skills as you're learning them.
www.powerpromote.com – once you have a website up and running, use this site to promote it.
www.geocities.com – free Web space for non-commercial sites. Together with a step-by-step guide, this is a brilliant start for the pupil who wants his or her own website.
www.arttoday.com – download all sorts of graphics to brighten up your web page for free!
www.imagitek.com/hex – whilst this site doesn't list all 16 million possible colours with their hexadecimal codes, it lists a fair few.
www.nedesign.com/colour – not quite sure what shade grey 7 is? Visit this site and test it out and, while you're there, experiment with a few colour combinations.
www.pagedoctor.com – download lots of freebies including animations.
www.globalgold.co.uk – register your own domain name.

Books

Build your own website (Usborne Computer Guides).

What is it?

E-mail, short for electronic mail, is the ability to send messages across the Internet from your computer to any other person who has an e-mail address.

How it works

When an e-mail message is sent, it is routed around the Internet by computers known as mail servers. These make sure that your e-mail reaches its destination computer. If the recipient's computer is not switched on, the e-mail will be stored on their mail server until they next check their e-mail. As soon as the recipient logs on and opens their e-mail program, the message should appear in their incoming mailbox ready to be opened and read.

General advantages of e-mail

● It's far faster than sending a letter, and distance is no object.
● The cost of sending an e-mail is that of a local phone call regardless of whether it's going to Boston or Birmingham.
● The same message can be sent simultaneously to any number of people.

E-mail has many advantages in the educational context. Its style is generally informal and consists of fairly short pieces of prose. It is therefore an excellent vehicle for the slow or reluctant writer, or for pupils with disabilities – the fact that they may have struggled to create even a few lines of text does not show in the result. The real sense of audience is a great motivational factor for the writer, and the general speed of response is also a good motivator, with feedback being more immediate and rewarding than the postal system (often referred to as snail mail).

Anatomy of an e-mail address

All e-mail addresses are unique, much like telephone numbers. They consist of a user name and a domain name. In the address *freddie@aol.com*, for example, the user has chosen simply to be *freddie* – this is the user name, and he can be reached via a company called AOL, whose domain name is *aol.com.*

Writing an e-mail

E-mail can provide an opportunity to mail the same message to a single individual or more than one person. An e-mail is normally brief, informal and instantaneous.

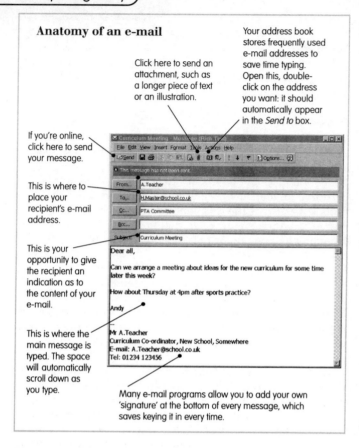

Anatomy of an e-mail

Your address book stores frequently used e-mail addresses to save time typing. Open this, double-click on the address you want: it should automatically appear in the *Send to* box.

Click here to send an attachment, such as a longer piece of text or an illustration.

If you're online, click here to send your message.

This is where to place your recipient's e-mail address.

This is your opportunity to give the recipient an indication as to the content of your e-mail.

This is where the main message is typed. The space will automatically scroll down as you type.

Many e-mail programs allow you to add your own 'signature' at the bottom of every message, which saves keying it in every time.

Mailing lists

Mailing lists are discussion groups that communicate with each other using e-mails. The discussions are not in real time as with IRC, and they differ from newsgroups in that messages are sent directly to participants as opposed to being posted on a bulletin board. A slight variation on this type of discussion-based mailing list is the announcement list. Here, periodic e-mails will be sent to people who have expressed an interest in the list's topic. The communication is therefore one way as opposed to two way. To join a mailing list, you first have to find one that you are interested in and then, using your e-mail program, follow the instructions provided by the mailing list.

Sending attachments

One useful feature of sending e-mails is the ability to send attachments. An attachment is a computer file which may take the form of a picture, photograph, video file, sound file or text file. The advantage is that the file will keep its original formatting and (assuming the recipient has suitable software to open it), they will receive it in the same format. When attaching a file you will need to know the name of the file you wish to send and its location on your hard disk.

E-mail netiquette

Activities undertaken on the Internet have developed 'unofficial' codes of practice. A number of points need to be remembered as regards sending e-mails:

- Always remember to include a suitable subject line.
- Always reply promptly if you can.
- Keep messages fairly brief and downloads to a manageable size – a large download may incur considerable expense to the recipient.
- Keep formatting to a minimum as it rarely stays intact.
- Never include a signature more than four lines long.

Emoticons

While e-mails are often written in a conversational style, they are actually very rudimentary conversational vehicles. Indeed, as a means of communication an e-mail is fairly basic. It is based on plain, informal text devoid of any non-verbal messages which can at times prove very limiting. Even a telephone conversation, which takes place without visual contact, is reliant on many factors other than the words being spoken. Pauses, tonal changes and the high incidence of incomplete words and sentences are all very much characteristic of a successful telephone conversation. 'Emoticons', more commonly known as 'smileys', therefore are used to help insert a modicum of emotion.

Below are a few examples. Note that they are all made using only the keys on your keyboard and they are meant to be viewed sideways:

:-) – *happy*	:'-(– *crying*	:-(– *sad*	:-o – *surprised*

Acronyms

To save time typing long messages, a list of commonly used acronyms has been built up. Whilst a little confusing at first, they can speed things up significantly. Below are a few examples:

BFN Bye For Now	*TTYL Talk To You Later*
FYI For Your Information	*OTOH On The Other Hand*
IMHO In My Humble Opinion	*B4 Before*

Why you need to know these facts

One of the key additions to the National Curriculum for ICT (2000) has been the inclusion of e-mail (ICT 2,3a). Indeed e-mail, along with the World Wide Web, is one of the most popular features of the Internet. You can correspond with other primary schools locally, even on the other side of the world (bearing different time zones in mind). You could then exchange information about the weather, local customs, swap data on popular projects. Setting up a correspondence with local secondary schools can also make transition less intimidating for Year 6 pupils.

Amazing facts

● Did you know that e-mail has an official birthday? It was 'born' on October 20th 1969.
● An e-mail sent across the world to Australia may reach its destination within one minute.

Common misconceptions

You need a computer to send an e-mail.
You do not need a computer to send e-mail. New technologies are making it possible to send e-mails using, among other things, TVs and mobile phones.

E-mails are private.
E-mails are not as private as you may want them to be. Never write anything in an e-mail you would not like anybody else to read, and make sure your password is kept a secret to minimize the risk of other people reading your messages or sending them on your behalf.

Handy tips

● Enter e-mail addresses into your address book. This facility should be available to you with your e-mail program, and will cut down on time spent entering e-mail addresses.
● Compose and read e-mails offline to cut down on telephone costs.
● If you wish to test whether your e-mail is working, send yourself a message.
● Remember that e-mail is best restricted to short pieces of unformatted text. If you wish to send anything more substantial, send it as an attachment.
● If you're not sure which type of word processor a person has and you wish to send them a text file, save your

document as a plain text (.txt) or Rich Text Format (.rtf) file. Both should be accessible to most word processors, though there may still be inconsistencies regarding formatting.

● Once opened, e-mails can be retrieved and re-read without you having to be online.

● Make sure you delete old e-mails once you are sure they are no longer needed, otherwise they will take up valuable space on your computer.

What's the difference between a carbon copy (cc) and a blind carbon copy (bcc)?
The carbon copy facility allows the sender to send one e-mail to many people at once. A party invitation or a New Year's greeting may be one example where this might be appropriate. A blind carbon copy does the same, but the reader of your e-mail is unable to see the names of the other recipients.

Will I miss e-mails if my computer is switched off?
No, when you are away from your computer, or not connected to the Internet, your e-mails will be safely stored on a mail server by your ISP. As soon as you go online this will be detected and your waiting e-mail will be directed to your mailbox.

The motivational aspects of e-mail communication makes it an excellent vehicle for use in the classroom. The problem for the teacher when planning sessions based on e-mail is finding suitable recipients. Organizations such as Kidlink are an excellent starting place. These can help build up links with a particular school anywhere else in the world and find a class to communicate with. However, unless a purposeful dialogue is established, interactions will soon lose momentum.

A living story
Try starting a 'live story' project. Here pupils from each participating class or school take it in turns to build up a story. Daily printouts of the story so far can be read out to the whole class and individuals take it in turns to add to the story. Dialogue between teachers before the actual start of the project needs to consider issues such as genre, and whether the story should take a fairytale, thriller, suspense or soap-opera format. Consider whether it should be written in the style of a particular author.

Express yourself

Introduce pupils to the concept of smileys. After giving a few examples, let pupils create their own. Pupils will be surprised how much non-verbal communication takes place and how easily misinterpretations can happen. How we say something is often just as important as what we are saying. Smileys aim to convey just how something was said.

Acronyms

Discuss some of the more useful acronyms that pupils may use. Give pupils a piece of text you have prepared in advance using some known and some unknown acronyms. Let pupils translate the text. As an extension activity, ask pupils to come up with ideas of their own.

Vocabulary

Flame mail – aggressive mail.
Shouting – messages written in capital letters.
Snail mail – mail sent by the traditional postal system.
Spamming – sending a barrage of unwanted e-mails to a person or newsgroup.
Bounce – when an e-mail cannot be delivered (maybe because you mis-typed an e-mail address), it will bounce back to you.
Smiley – a face used to convey emotion in an e-mail, made up using characters on a keyboard.
Mailbox – used to store e-mails.

Resources

Useful webites

www.onelist.com – a community of mailing lists with an opportunity to set up your own.
www.eduweb.co.uk – you can access *Netpals* from this site. Pupils fill out a short form about themselves and are accepted onto the database. (Rejections are occasionally made, but should usually be explained.) To find a netpal pupils fill out a questionnaire stating their preferences and then wait for a response.
http://rite.ed.qut.edu.au./oz-teachernet/projects/travel-buddies/ – Travel Buddies is an Australian scheme where primary schools across the world send each other a soft toy, take it everywhere with them and send back a log describing its adventures.

ICT
Glossary

Absolute cell – cell reference in a spreadsheet whose value and position in formulae does not change.

ADSL – Asymmetric Digital Subscriber Line. A new, high-speed digital telephone line.

Algorithm – a prepared piece of code that is used frequently. Most programmers have a selection of algorithms that can be used instead of rewriting time-consuming code from scratch.

Amend – to change or alter a record.

Append – to add new data to a database from another, already existing source.

Application – a piece of software installed on a computer to perform a specific function.

Archive – a file that is stored in a compressed state to save space.

ARPA – Advanced Research Projects Agency.

Autotracing – the process of converting a bitmap image into a vector image.

Background printing – a feature that allows you to carry on working while a document is printing.

Back-up – to make a copy of important files on floppy disk or other storage device.

BASIC – Beginner's All-purpose Symbolic Instruction Code.

Baud rate – speed at which a modem can send information down a telephone line, measured in Kbps.

BBS – Bulletin Board System.

Beta – new version of software that is still being tested.

Bitmap – type of picture whereby the image is comprised of a finite number of differently coloured dots (pixels).

Bounce – when an e-mail cannot be delivered (maybe because e-mail address has been mistyped), it will 'bounce' back to you.

Browser – Piece of software used for browsing the World Wide Web.

Bug – an error in a program's code that causes the program to function incorrectly.

Bundled software – software that comes with the purchase of a new computer. Often called OEM (Original Equipment Manufacturer) software.

Cache – a type of memory where frequently used items of data are stored; cache memory is more expensive than normal memory.

CAD – Computer Aided Design.

CCD – Charge Coupled Device.

CD-ROM – Compact Disc–Read-Only Memory.

CD-R – Compact Disc Recordable; CD that can be written to once only.
CD-RW – Compact Disc ReWritable; A blank CD that can be written to many times.
Cell – a single portion of a spreadsheet, used to hold a numeric value.
Client – a computer that accesses data from a server.
COBOL – COmmon Business Orientated Language.
Compression – reduction of the size of a file.
CPU – Central Processing Unit.
Crop – to cut off unwanted parts of a picture.
CRT – Cathode Ray Tube. The part of a monitor that displays the image.

Database – a searchable, structured collection of information stored on a computer that can be accessed in a number of ways.
Data logging – using a computer to automatically measure variables such as light, sound and heat.
Data transfer time – the time taken to transfer data from CD-ROM to the computer.
Debugging – correcting errors in a program's code.
Desktop – the digital version of a desk where icons for files, folders and programs can be arranged.
DIMM – Dual In-line Memory Modules. Used by later Pentiums and all Pentium II and Pentium III processors.
DIP – Digital Image Processing.
DNS – Domain Name System.
Docking station – required by a notebook to connect to a desktop PC.
Domain name – the 'address' of a website; used to locate a page on the World Wide Web.
Download – to copy files from another computer on the Internet to your own computer.
dpi – Dots Per Inch.
Driver – software that communicates between the computer and a peripheral device such as a printer.
Dumb terminal – a computer programmed to carry out one function or task, such as an electronic word processor.
DVD – Digital Versatile Disc.

e-commerce – buying goods and services online.
e-mail – electronic mail; the sending of text from one person to another over the Internet.

Flame mail – aggressive mail.
Flat file database – simple one-file database structure.
Freeware – software provided with no charge for its usage.
FTP – File Transfer Protocol. A system which allows you to transfer files from a computer on the Internet to your own.
FTP client – a program needed to upload your files to your host computer.

GIF – Graphics Interchange Format. Type of graphic file commonly used on the Internet.
Grey scale – producing a picture using shades of grey.
GUI – Graphical User Interface. System of controlling a computer by means of visual representation of the functions of the computer.

Homepage – the first page of a website, rather like a welcome page.
Host computer – a host computer links a user's computer to the Internet.
Hotlist – a summative list of hits constructed by a search engine in response to a specific search.
HTML – HyperText Mark-up Language. The language used to write web pages.
Hypertext links – words or pictures that are highlighted or underlined to show that they link to other pages or sites; when you point to a hypertext link with your mouse, the pointer will change to a pointing finger symbol. Also known as hyperlinks.
Hz (Hertz) – the measurement of a monitor's refresh rate.

Icon – an image on screen representing a program, file, folder or particular function.
Interface – a device used to connect two separate devices together.
Internet Service Providers – companies that provide access to the Internet via powerful host computers. Otherwise known as ISPs.
Intranet – miniature network, similar in function to the Internet but accessible only

to computers on the immediate local network; often referred to as a 'walled garden'.
IRC – Internet Relay Chat. Form of real-time discussion carried out over the Internet.
ISDN – Integrated Services Digital Network. A fast digital phone line often used to connect to the Internet.

Java – an advanced programming language used to add animations and interactivity to web pages.
Jaz disk – high-capacity storage medium from Iomega, often used for backing up data and transferring extremely large files.
JPEG – Joint Picture Experts Group. Type of highly compressed graphic file format seen frequently on the Internet.

K (Kilobyte) – the way we measure the size of a computer's memory; equivalent to 1024 bytes.
K/s – Kilobytes per second.
Kbps – Kilobits per second. The speed of data transmission of a modem is measured in Kbps (or Mbps – Megabits per second).
Kerning – refers to the space between individual letters.

LAN – Local Area Network.
LCD – Liquid Crystal Display.
Leading – refers to the spacing between lines of text.
Leased line – a permanent telephone line connection to the Internet.
Legend – similar to a key used for charts and graphs.
Line art – an image made up only of lines, without shading.
Local links – hyperlinks within a website.

Mailbox – used to store e-mails.
Match – a record which satisfies the query conditions.
Mb (Megabyte) – measure of data storage, equivalent to 1024K.
Menu – a list of possible options.
MHz – measure of how fast a computer's CPU can work, in MegaHertz.
Modem – MOdulator/DEModulator: a device to connect computers via telephone lines.
Moderated newsgroup – a newsgroup where all postings are checked by

moderators before being published.
Morphing – the process of one image gradually turning into another.
MS-DOS – MicroSoft–Disk Operating System.

NIC – Network Information Centre. This controls the use of domain names, ensuring that each particular domain name is only used once.
Node – another name for a computer that is connected to a network, more commonly referred to as a workstation.

OCR – Optical Character Recognition.
Offline – not connected to the Internet.
OLE – Object Linking and Embedding.
Online – connected to the Internet.
Operating System – the central program controlling the operation of a computer and its peripheral devices; for example Microsoft Windows.

PC – Personal Computer.
PDF – Portable Document Format.
Pentium – name for the microchip developed by Intel.
Picture Frame – box used to position picture on a page.
Pixel – smallest point in an image.
Plug and play – new technology that makes the installation of new equipment much simpler.
Print server – a machine dedicated to controlling print jobs for the network.
Programming – writing computer programs.
PPM – speed of printing, measured in Pages Per Minute.

Query – specifies certain conditions which the database program has to match when searching.

RAM – Random Access Memory.
Record – a collection of related fields.
Refresh rate – the number of times the picture on a screen is redrawn each second.
Relational database – rather than having one large database file it is often more efficient to have two or more separate but related files. For example, a school might have a pupils' details database with an additional relational database file

Glossary

concerned with pupils' exam results. For the two files to be linked, at least one field should be the same, the key field; in this case the obvious one is name.

Relative Cell – cell on a spreadsheet whose location changes in relation to the location of the formula referring to it.

Remote link – hyperlinks to sites other than your own.

Resolution – the clarity of a screen image, determined by the number of pixels displayed, measured in dpi.

Rollerball – method of directional input similar to that of a mouse.

ROM – Read-Only Memory.

Scanner – device that allows images to be 'captured' from printed form to a digital form that can be manipulated on a computer.

SDRAM – the latest type of DIMM memory module.

Search engine – a program that searches the World Wide Web for pages of information on a specific topic.

Seek time – the amount of time taken by laser beam to locate data on a CD-ROM.

Sensor – a monitoring device that measures physical changes and sends corresponding data back to the processor, usually via an interface.

Serial and parallel ports – the connectors at the back of the CPU, which are used to plug in peripheral devices.

Server – a powerful computer that stores, sorts and distributes data on the Internet.

Shareware – a program that can be trialled by the user for free before they decide whether to purchase the software.

Shouting – e-mail messages written in capital letters.

SIMM – Single In-line Memory Module. These come in two sizes: 30-pin and 72-pin. The 30-pin modules are mainly used by older 386 and 486 processors; the 72-pin modules are used by newer 486 and early Pentium processors.

Smiley – a face used to convey emotion in an e-mail, made up using characters on a keyboard, for example ;-). Also known as emoticons.

Snail mail – mail sent by the traditional postal system.

Sort – to organize data in order of, for example, size or frequency.

Spamming – sending unwanted e-mails to a person or newsgroup.

Surfing – used to describe exploration of the Internet.

TAN – Total Area Network.

TCP – Transmission Control Protocol. A standard of communication that has been established so that all computers on the Internet 'speak' the same language.

Text wrap – the ability to place text around an object.

Text frame – box to hold text on a page.

TFT – Thin Film Transistor. A type of flat screen monitor often found in laptops.

Thumbnail – postage stamp sized image.

TIFF – high-quality image file format.

Time interval – time between individual readings when data logging.

UNIX – an alternative operating system to MS-DOS.

Upload – to copy files from your own computer to another computer on the Internet.

URL – Uniform Resource Locator. The address which identifies a website.

USB port – Universal Serial Bus; this is the new standard for connecting peripherals to a computer.

Vector – type of graphic comprising scalable geometric shapes rather than individual pixels.

Virus – piece of unsolicited code that is deliberately designed to cause damage to a computer.

WAN – Wide Area Network.

Web browser – software required to surf the Internet.

Webmaster – the person responsible for creating and managing a website.

Windows CE – a cut-down version of Microsoft's Windows operating system used by hand-held computers.

WWW – World Wide Web. A collection of interactive pages found on the Internet.

WYSIWYG – What You See Is What You Get, meaning that the program can print an exact copy of the screen image.

Zip drive – a high-capacity disk drive designed by Iomega.

Zipped file – a compressed file.

ICT
Index